The
NORTH
SUNDERLAND RAILWAY

THE
NORTH SUNDERLAND RAILWAY

by
Alan Wright

THE OAKWOOD PRESS

© 1988 Oakwood Press and Alan Wright

ISBN 0 85361 335 4

Printed by Netherwood Dalton & Co. Ltd., Huddersfield

First Edition October 1967
Second Enlarged Edition 1988

Acknowledgements

I would like to acknowledge the help I have received from all those who have supplied snippets of information which have fitted together and helped to fill in the story. Since the first edition of this history considerable material has been received from many people. It is impossible to list all those who have helped me, but I must record my thanks to my daughter Janet who never knew the railway but who has typed the manuscript, and the late Bill Tate of Sale who loved the railway and to whom I dedicate this work.

Published by
The OAKWOOD PRESS
P.O.Box 122, Headington, Oxford.

Contents

"All change" for the North Sunderland Railway   *Author's Collection*

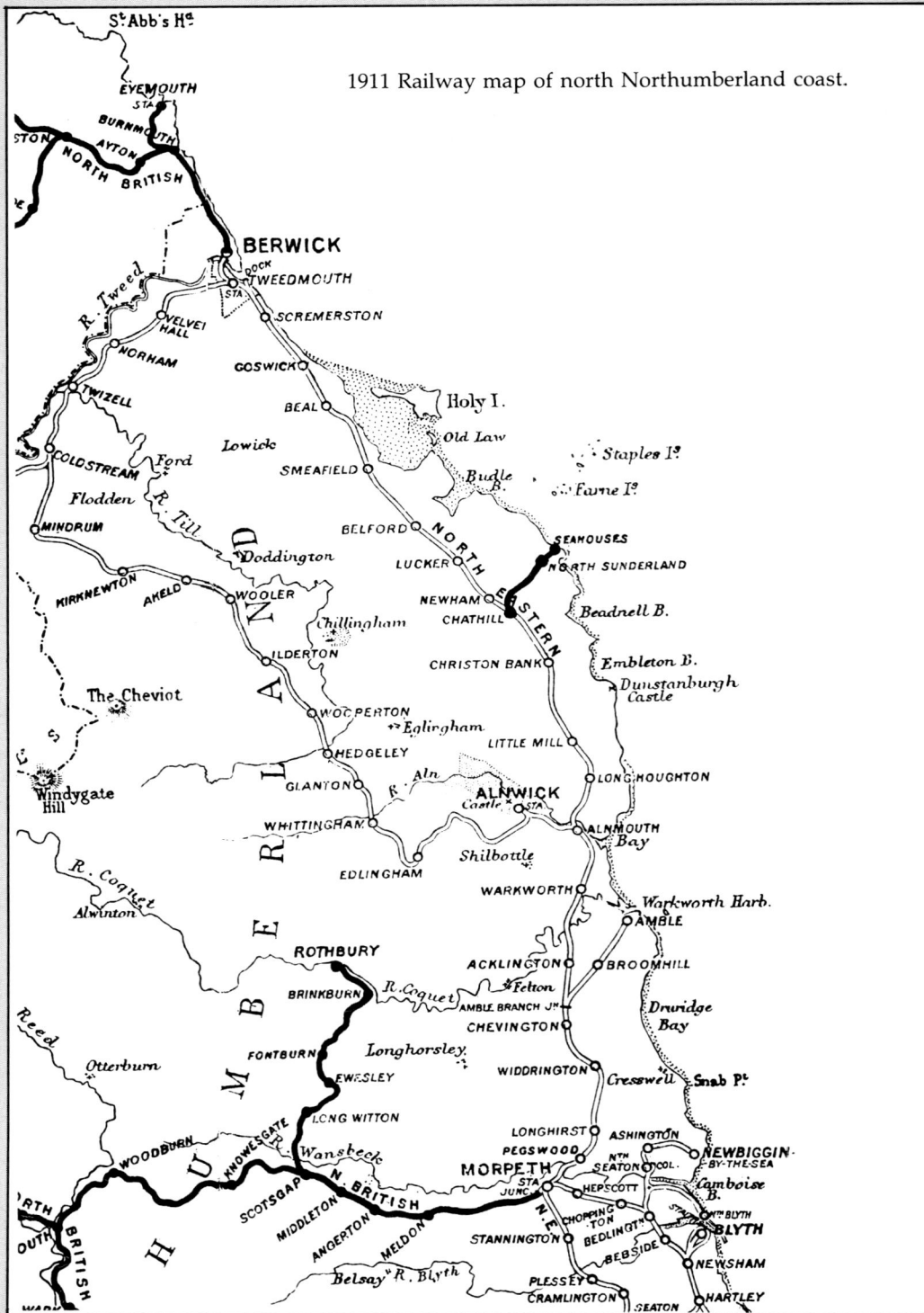

1911 Railway map of north Northumberland coast.

Introduction

The North Sunderland Railway in its working days was not particularly well known beyond its immediate environs. The railway enthusiasts of the day paid it scant attention, and the few photographers concentrating on railway subjects presumably were loathe to take their cumbersome equipment to photograph "the funny little train".

With construction under way in line with an Act of Parliament obtained before the passing of legislation which permitted the creation of "light railways", the Company nevertheless sought powers under a Light Railway Order to simplify its construction and raise finances for an extension which was never built.

Throughout its working life the Company was known by its title, the North Sunderland Railway. Only after the ending of its services, and in an endeavour to save a costly Act of Parliament to enable it to be wound up, was the Company changed to a limited liability company with the registered title of "The North Sunderland Light Railway Company Limited".

Unfortunately many of today's railway historians, who never knew the North Sunderland Railway, or who have not researched its past, will insist on calling it by its wrong name to the dismay of all those who knew and loved it with all its idiosyncracies. It is hoped this story will revive many pleasant memories of that "most important railway to which the North Eastern was but a mere feeder".

Alan Wright
Newton-le-Willows
September 1987

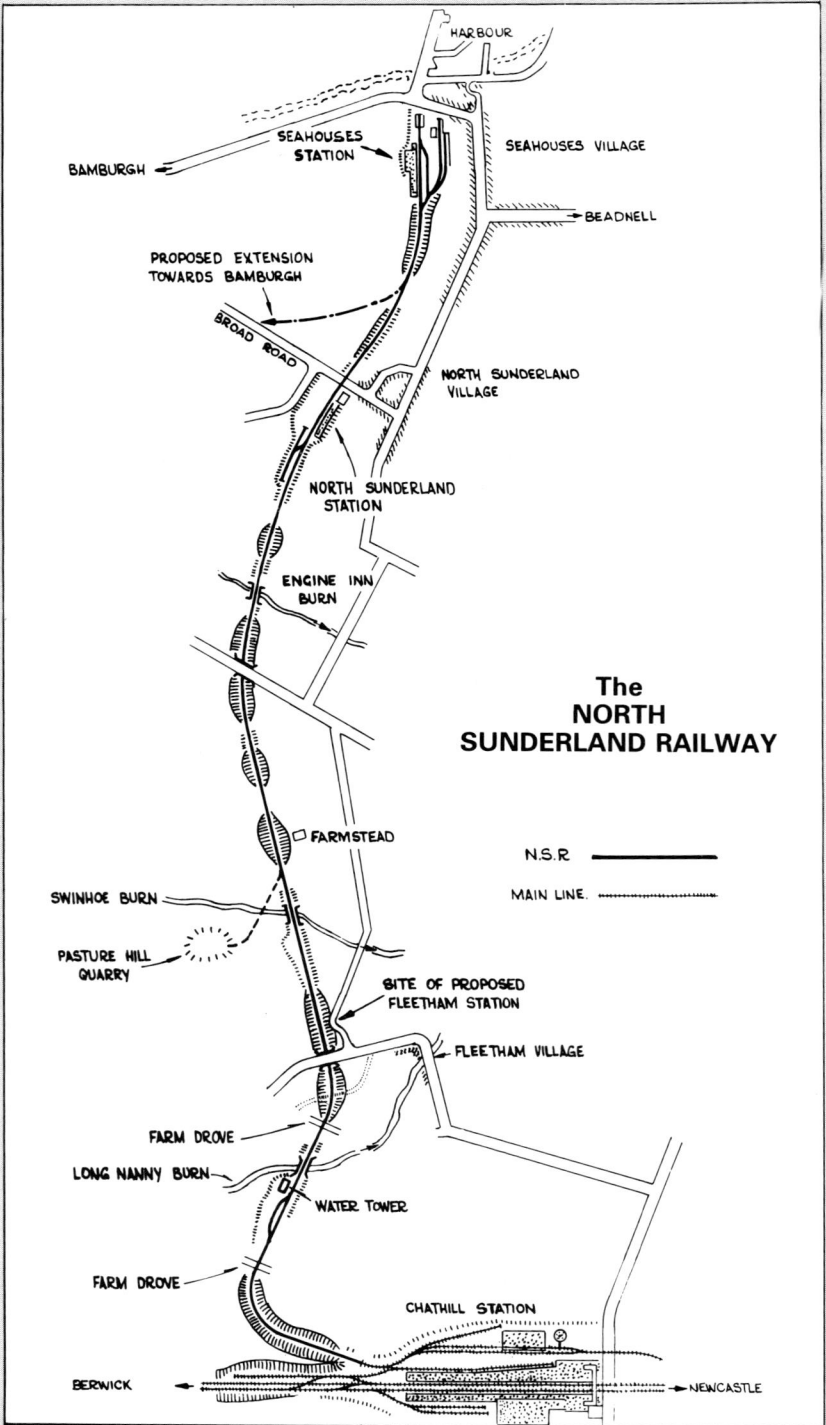

Map of the Railway with reference to features mentioned in text.

Chapter One

The Company is formed

To many people the mention of Northumberland, until recent years, conjured up a mental picture of a bleak, unfriendly part of the country covered by collieries and populated by a barbaric horde descended from the Norseman.

Thanks to a very active Northumbria Tourist Board this old image has been shaken off to be replaced by one of sand, castles, beautiful hills and moorland scenery, in short a tourist's paradise. Many of the people discovering Northumbria come eventually to the little fishing village of Seahouses to see, amongst other things, the Farne Islands lying just off the coast and to make the short voyage from Seahouses harbour to the islands in one of the little fishing boats. No doubt, when parking their car in the large car park behind Main Street, the visitors do not know that they are in the one time station yard of the North Sunderland Railway whose single track made its way westwards to Chathill on the east coast main line.

Many famous names are associated with Northumberland, names such as Stephenson, Armstrong, Bewick, Collingwood and Grace Darling. The early days of Christianity in this country were cradled in Northumberland; in the 7th Century a cathedral was built at Holy Island under the auspices of St Aidan, Bishop of Lindisfarne. In the period 660–670 St Cuthbert became the Prior of Lindisfarne, but in 676 he went to live as a recluse on the Inner Farne, where he eventually died in March 687.

The Northumbrian coast in this area is a mixture of rocky bays and stretches of firm golden sand; Holy Island is reached from the mainland by a causeway which is impassable twice a day. The Farnes are a group of rocky islands inhabited by sea-birds. The castle at Bamburgh is one of a chain built throughout Northumberland and, standing atop its mound, is a well-known landmark. Its picture is often a reminder of home to many exiled Northumbrians.

In the reign of Queen Elizabeth I, Sir John Foster was made the Governor of Bamburgh Castle and his grand-daughter, one Dorothy Foster, married Nathaniel, Lord Crewe, Bishop of Durham who bought the Bamburgh Estate, the Castle, the North Sunderland Estate and the Blanchland Estate near Hexham. In his will of June 1720 Lord Crewe formed a charity trust which made grants to various charitable and educational bodies and the balance went to the benefit of necessitous clergy in the two dioceses of Durham and Newcastle. After the end of the regime of Lord Crewe's trust the castle was bought by the first Lord Armstrong who so splendidly restored it to its present state.

7

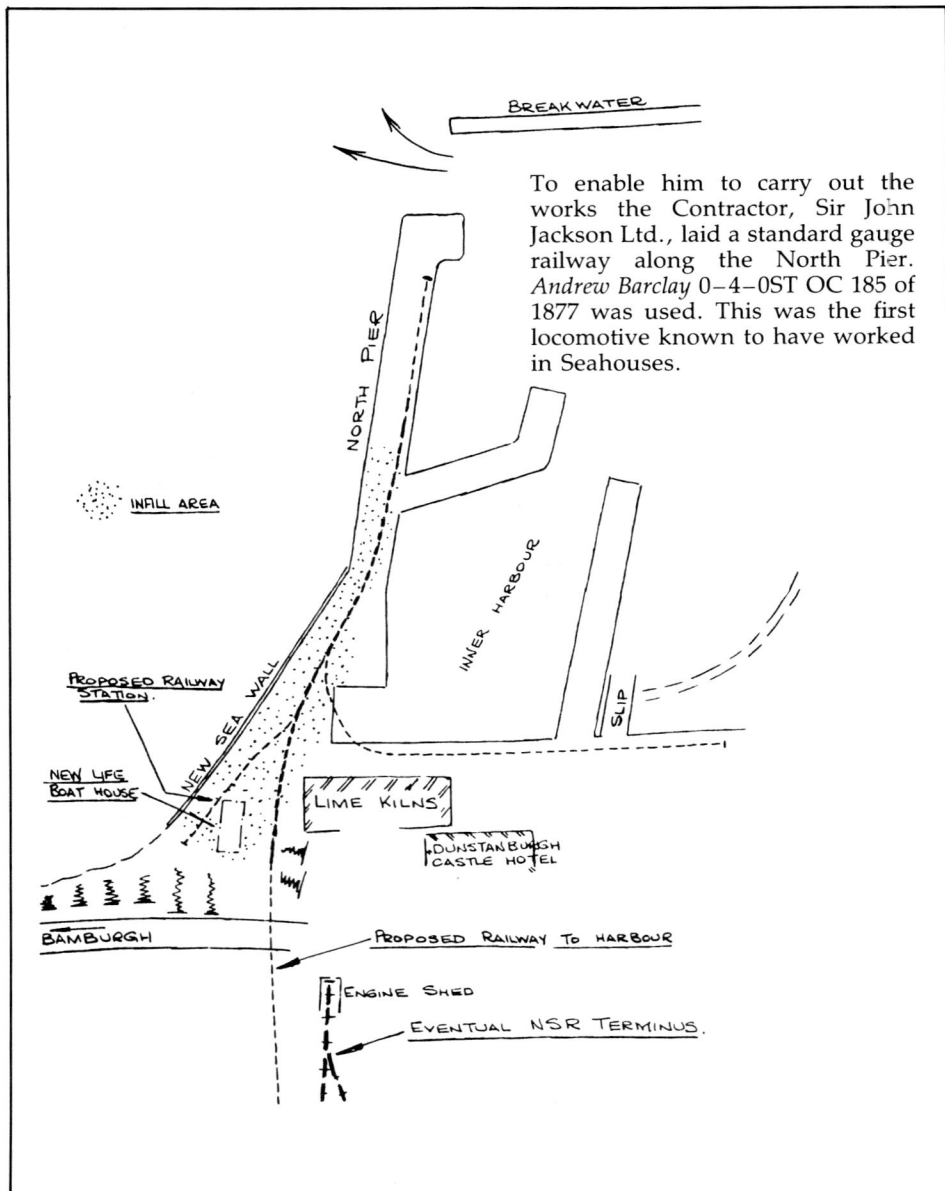

To enable him to carry out the works the Contractor, Sir John Jackson Ltd., laid a standard gauge railway along the North Pier. *Andrew Barclay* 0–4–0ST OC 185 of 1877 was used. This was the first locomotive known to have worked in Seahouses.

Seahouses harbour works showing Contractor's railway.

Some three miles south of Bamburgh lies the village of North Sunderland and its near neighbour on the coast, Seahouses, or – to give it its old name – North Sunderland Seahouses. The origin of North Sunderland is interesting, in old documents it is known as Sutherland meaning the land south of Bamburgh within the estate. Through time this was corrupted to Sunderland and the "North" was added later to avoid confusion with the other Sunderland on Wearside.

Most of the land in the area belonged to Lord Crewe's Trustees who built a small harbour at Seahouses to give protection from the storms in the North Sea to the villagers' fishing boats. Only a small harbour, it served its purpose adequately for many years. However, in the 1870s, the Trustees decided to enlarge the harbour so that it would be capable of giving shelter to a large number of steam and sailing ships which, at that time, could only run for the Tyne or the Forth when gales and rough seas blew up.

After much discussion it was eventually decided to construct a new north pier and a seaward breakwater at a cost of approximately £30,000. The necessary Parliamentary consent was sought under the Pier and Harbour Order Confirmation Act of 1885. This document set out the scale of charges to be levied for the handling of a multitude of export and import cargoes from and to all parts of the world. It also granted the Harbour Commissioners, to whom the control of the harbour would eventually pass, the right to give licences for the operation of steam tugs and the provision of pilots! In the end the contract for the modest works creating the harbour of today was let to Mr (later Sir) John Jackson, who carried out the work during 1886 to 1888. He constructed a standard gauge railway on the pier to carry rock brought from Blyth by barge to where it was required on the north pier where a timber framework was infilled and a concrete shell applied to it. The work cost £31,189 2s. 8d.. To operate the railway the contractor used an Andrew Barclay saddle tank locomotive which no doubt was also brought in and removed by sea. This was the first locomotive to work in Seahouses.

Whilst the work was only carried out in 1886–1888, a map of 1879 produced during the early discussions on the harbour works showed a railway station to be built near the present lifeboat station with an incline up to the route later adopted.

The consultant engineers for the harbour works were Messrs J. Watt, Sanderson and Montcrieff of Newcastle.

It will be noticed that Lord Crewe's Trustees appreciated the importance of a rail link to the North Eastern Railway and approached that Company which did not have as much faith in the viability of the project as the Trustees. The North Eastern's main line was some four miles inland at Chathill, and the link obviously the means of getting goods to and from the harbour. A branch line would increase the prosperity of the village and the fishermen who had to carry their catches to Chathill over the rough unmetalled roads of the period. Similarly, incoming goods had to be transported to the coast.

As the North Eastern Railway was not showing any interest in the branch line scheme, the Trustees decided to go it alone by forming their own Company and, as a result, called a public meeting in the Drill Hall at Seahouses on Saturday 11th April, 1891. Under the chairmanship of Mr James Ewing the various factors in promoting a line were discussed and eventually it was decided to go ahead with the scheme. A local newspaper reported the proceedings fully under the heading "Northumbrian Fishing Stations. Development of the North Sunderland Trade. Proposed Branch Railway".

The report stated that:

> . . . It is a good five miles by road from North Sunderland Harbour to Chathill, and along this road the fish brought into the harbour have to be carted before they can be put on the rails for market. Under such circumstances it is not surprising that there is a clamour for a branch line of railway which will enable the fishermen to pack their produce into trucks on the quayside and despatch it without further trouble to its various destinations. Not only would this additional facility of transit be a saving in the cost and trouble at present necessary but it would, it is believed, be a great factor in bringing more fishing boats to this little Northumbrian port where there is plenty of room for the development of the trade. The fishers are hard-working people in this isolated village. They show an almost sullen determination under very trying conditions to keep the wolf from the door and fight poverty with the same amount of undaunted ferocity as their ancient ancestry did more tangible foes for they are said to be direct descendents of the Vikings. Yet it is certain that they by no means live in luxury, and, if the time and expense involved in the cartage of their fish could be saved, it would go a considerable way towards improving their means of obtaining a decent livelihood. This, as is natural, seems to be the most pressing reason for the formation of a new railway. Another reason is that North Sunderland would become a watering place of no inconsiderable attractions, and, through the circulation of the visitors' money, they might be able to add a few comforts to their present very frugal habits of life.
>
> The natural beauties of the place are great and with reasonable facilities for reaching it there is no doubt it would be improved in many respects. The railway project has frequently been considered and seems to be the only means devisable by which the present state of affairs can be bettered.
>
> A meeting of the inhabitants of the neighbourhood was held in the Drill Hall at Seahouses on Saturday for the purpose of considering the scheme. Mr James Ewing, Fish curer, North Sunderland, presided and among those present were County Alderman the Rev. D. Dixon Brown; County

Councillor G.D. Atkinson Clark; Lieut-Col. Marshall; Captain Simmonds; Mr Charles Percy, Coroner for North Northumberland; Rev. Leonard Shafto Orde of Shoreston; County Councillor R. Burdon Sanderson; Mr James Sanderson; Mr George Wilson sen.; Mr William King; and others. There was a large attendance.

The Chairman, at the opening of the proceedings, said he had received letters from several gentlemen. County Councillor Howey-Taylor wrote that he would do anything he could to urge upon the North Eastern Railway to run a line to accommodate the coast villagers and North Sunderland would be the greatest factor in inducing the company to listen to the appeal. In his experience he had always found that railway companies only listened to two reasons for laying down a line. The first was: would the traffic hold out a good chance of a reasonable return for outlay and working expenses; and secondly, whether there was a good chance for the company to take the matter up. He might also mention that there was a rush for seaside resorts all along the Northumberland coast.

Messrs David Cochrane and Company, fish curers, Leith, in a letter said that if they could get a rate by rail about 1s. 3d. per barrel it would be an inducement to send a large quantity of their herrings by rail instead of sea as they would save dues both at Leith and at North Sunderland. It would also be much more convenient if a line were laid down to Seahouses thereby giving facilities for the despatch of fish to market. There would be every reason to believe that deep sea fishing in the winter would be developed greatly as probably many of the Scotch boats would, instead of going farther south, take North Sunderland as a nearer and thereby more convenient place. They trusted the people of Sea Houses [sic] would be able speedily to begin operations. (Hear, hear) Mr George Woodger (of Messrs John Woodger and Sons, Yarmouth, Newcastle, etc.) also wrote to the effect that he was convinced that unless they got railway communication Sea Houses [sic] would be a place of the past. There had been such a change in the fishing trade during the last 10 years that fishermen, unless compelled, would not use a harbour that had no railway communication. It would bring more buyers and boats to the harbour, and plenty of visitors for pleasure. (Applause)

The Chairman, continuing his speech, said he thought they would all be of one opinion, that they really needed railway communication with the main line, and that as speedily as possible. From the data he had to lay before them he was sorry that he could not prove that such a line would be a success at once but they had every reason to believe that with a very little development they would certainly be able to double their quantities. He had calculated the estimated tonnage between North Sunderland and Chathill with the following results:

Coals	about 1500 tons
Herrings, kippers, cured and fresh	about 1600 tons
White fish produce, etc.	150 tons
Bait for the fishermen	50 tons
Manure	190 tons
Acid, etc.	100 tons

General parcels, goods, etc.	150 tons
Grain, potatoes, cattle and sheep	
(from farms nearer Sea Houses [sic] than Chathill)	450 tons

a total of 4190 tons. Between Beadnell and Seahouses the estimate was 1100, bringing the grand total up to 5290 tons. He had very little data for passenger traffic but at present they would probably have 6000 and 7000 passengers and that would be the very first item that would extend. With respect to North Sunderland as a summer resort and bathing place, with their famous Shoreston Sands he thought it could not be beaten, and there could easily be 30 or 40 very respectable villa residences erected at a moderate cost.

Even in the near future they might have a very considerable extension of trade in coal and lime, He saw no reason why the lime works should not be started again. Then they might take in as a probability that they might run the line to Beadnell and take both the villages in and develop them as bathing places. He thought their trade might very easily double itself if only they had the railway brought down to them, and if in the near future it could be seen that North Sunderland Harbour could be deepened by 5 ft, it would not at all be a difficult thing to prophesy, with every promise of fulfilment, knowing that their quantities would soon rise to 50,000 tons. (*Applause*) The trawlers, knowing that they could get their fish straight to market, might often advantageously come into North Sunderland instead of returning to Newcastle or Shields. (*Hear, hear.*)

Mr George Wilson, sen., proposed the following resolution:

That this meeting of the inhabitants of North Sunderland Sea Houses [*sic*] and District is of the opinion that a railway connection between North Sunderland Harbour and the North Eastern main line is necessary to the commercial success and development of the district and that such a connecting line would ultimately prove financially successful. (*Applause*)

There could be no doubt, he said, as to the urgent need there was in the district for railway accommodation. North Sunderland – North Shields excepted – was by far the most important fishing station on the coast. Notwithstanding that, they were more unfavourably situated and more isolated from railway communication than any of the other fishing stations. He was rather afraid that they had not a strong case to put before the railway directors but he was sanguine enough to believe that with a branch line the fishing trade would develop by leaps and bounds, the prospects were encouraging. They had a splendid harbour and, directly in front of them, one of the most productive fishing grounds on the North Coast, then at North Sunderland they had a Marine Promenade with a seascape and a bit of coast line which he thought was not excelled in beauty on any other part of the coast. That would attract a great number of visitors if there were easy facilities for reaching the place, and altogether he thought the scheme would ultimately prove successful. (*Applause*)

Mr William King seconded the motion and alluded to the fact that all the white fish and herring which came into the harbour were caught immediately off the place. North Shields was good enough as a harbour but they, too, wanted railway communication with their market.

County Councillor G.D.A. Clark gave some information respecting the cost, etc., of constructing railways generally. He said that no Northumbrian could with equanimity see that those fishing villages on their coast were rapidly becoming depopulated, and from a national point of view still less so. They could not with equanimity see those schools for the navy and the merchant service and the sources of the national food supply being diminished. No industry could possibly flourish unless it had ready means of despatching its produce to the markets at which it was saleable, and that seemed to be the greatest difficulty in regard to the Northumberland coast. Now, if the North Eastern Company would take up the question of a line from Chathill to North Sunderland it would very much simplify matters, but he was rather afraid that at any rate in the first instance they would have to trust a little to local effort in any such enterprise. When he heard of the project he wrote to several places for information. Mr Wolfe Barry, who was a great engineer, rather threw cold water on his ideas when he told him that they might construct such a railway for £8000 to £10,000 a mile. He then went to the Board of Trade and got a number of blue books from Mr Courtney Boyle. From these he learnt that Irish Railways formed under the Act of 1883 cost over £4000 a mile. The procedure under that Act, however, was very cumbrous. These railways, moreover, were on the narrow gauge of three feet and a report which he had conclusively proved that a railway such as they intended must be laid down on the ordinary gauge of the country for the connections. (*Hear, hear.*) There was a line on the North [*sic*] Eastern Railway at Wisbech which seemed to him to be very much the sort of thing that they required. It was eight miles in length, four of which were on the public highway. The land cost £8000. There are three bridges on it, and the works cost £23,000, making a total of over £31,000. But the tramway proper, as it is called, ran up in various ways to £5,200 a mile. Of course, there were three bridges to be taken into consideration. The Board of Trade authorities had suggested to him that they should not call it a light railway but a tramway and the Board of Trade had power to allow them to construct such tramways. The real difficulty would be with the connections but that, he thought, could be got over if the railway company were with them. (*Applause*)

Capt Simmonds gave an outline of routes and estimated costs. He had gone over three routes he said and, in order not to be guided entirely by his own opinion, he had since forwarded the particulars to a well-known engineer who had checked all the figures and expressed himself satisfied that they were within the mark. The first route was leaving Chathill to Sea Houses, passing north of Fleetham and, adopting a curve rather than making a cutting, they could get in a distance of exactly four miles a very level line with no gradient exceeding 1 in 40 or 1 in 45 – 1 in 35 being a very practical limit. For a 3 ft gauge railway the cost per mile, including two stations, two small bridges, compensation for land, and provision for rolling stock including one locomotive, would be £2500 – a total of £10,500 for the whole length. The principal objection to that was the connection with the main line at Chathill, but taking the same route with a full sized gauge the cost would be as near as possible £3900, practically £16,000 for the whole length.

Another route with many more advantages included Swinhoe in the farming and Beadnell in the fishing interests. For this line he would leave Chathill by the north-east and curving round Fleetham, touch Swinhoe, on to Beadnell and past Anstead. Here a rather serious difficulty would crop up. They would either have to curve round the old quarries or they must bridge and cut through them. The cost for that would be much larger than the other. A 3 ft gauge line would cost £3000 a mile and a full gauge £4200 a mile. The total distance was 5½ miles. The third route was a modification of the second. It ran from Chathill, past Swinhoe and Beadnell, but having no station at Swinhoe and adopting a cutting instead of a curve at that place. The distance was practically the same but the mileage would cost £2900 instead of £3000 for a 3 ft gauge and £3900 instead of £4200 for a full gauge. He did not think that was as good as the second one. As to working, the chairman had given them a fair estimate. He (the speaker) calculated the traffic at 5000 tons as a maximum initial amount. At 1s. 3d. per ton, with 80 passengers a day at a shilling a piece and £100 for parcels in the year, there would be a total income for the first year of £1700. The working expenses, including station masters, posters, insurance, rates, etc would amount to £1200, leaving £500 profit on the first year's returns. (*Applause*) That on the capital first spent would return on the 3 ft gauge 4¾ per cent and on the full gauge 3¾ for the first route, and for the long route by Fleetham, Beadnell, and so on, on the 3 ft gauge it would return 3¾ per cent and on the full gauge 2¾ per cent. (*Applause*) No man, he thought, who had his head screwed on the right way could doubt that if the people of the coast chose to help themselves there was a good future before them. (*Hear, hear and applause.*)

Mr Charles Percy, in a short speech, said if the landed and commercial gentlemen and the fishermen whom he saw present were all interested he thought they might look forward to the time when the scheme would be an accomplished fact. Might they not get some assistance other than local? He looked forward to the time when local Councils would have the power of lending money to such schemes. If they could develop the trade of North Sunderland he thought any such railway would in the end pay a fair rate of interest. By deepening the harbour he thought they would greatly increase the trade. If the landowners and the railway company would meet the scheme in a public spirited manner he could see nothing to prevent it becoming successful. (*Applause*)

The Rev. D. Dixon-Brown, in addressing the meeting, agreed that if the railway had been suggested in Ireland with such a harbour in the neighbourhood it would be carried out at once. Because, unfortunately, they did not happen to live in Ireland, they would have to carry the agitation on until they got what they wanted. He came there that day as representing Lord Crewe's Trustees. He had not had an opportunity of speaking to them yet, but he hoped to do so on Tuesday when they held their half-yearly meeting. The projected line would probably have to pass through a great portion of the land owned by Lord Crewe's Trustees and he thought he might say they would give every facility for its formation. (*Applause*) As to the deepening of the harbour, they had gone to the utmost extent of their tether. The fishing trade had gone through a very serious change since the harbour works were built, and although he did not mean to say that work had been altogether a disappointment, they were not gaining that amount of revenue from the dues which they had expected. Under such circumstances they must wait for further development before they could spend more money. The Trustees were not looking for interest. What they wanted to do was to repay what they had borrowed. When they had reduced that, if they got any surplus for their revenues, they would be able to do something more. North Sunderland, he could not help thinking, would be an admirable watering place if they had railway communication and the Trustees would be ready – although they had no power to sell the land – to give all facilities for building that they could possibly do under the terms of the Trust. (*Applause*)

The motion was unanimously carried.

The Rev. Mr McPhee then moved the following resolution:

"That the following gentlemen be requested to form a deputation to the North Eastern Railway Company to ascertain their views respecting the formation of a branch line, and that the deputation be constituted a committee to further the scheme in every possible way: The Rev. D.D. Brown; Lieut-Col. Marshall; Captain Simmonds; Messrs John Craster; Howey-Taylor; Edmund Craster; George D. Atkinson Clarke; Captain Maugin; Charles Percy; H.A. Paynter; Rev. A.M. McPhee; George Wilson sen.; J.R. Johnson; James Ewing; James Scott; Edward Fordy; John Davidson; William King; Michael Robson; and Isaac Dixon."

Mr Nathan Woodger seconded the motion which was heartily adopted. A vote of thanks to speakers and chairman ended the meeting.

The deputation duly met the North Eastern Railway authorities who once again showed no interest in the project. Subsequently the gentlemen decided to proceed on their own and placed a Private Bill before Parliament. In 1892 Queen Victoria signed the North Sunderland Railway Act 1892.

This Act empowered the North Sunderland Railway Company to make and maintain in the lines, and according to the levels shown on the deposited plans and sections, the railway with all proper bridges, stations, sidings, approaches, junctions, roads, buildings, yards, works and conveniences associated therewith, and could enter upon, take, and use any such lands delineated on the plans and described in the book of plans.

The railways authorised in the Act were:

1 A railway four miles in length commencing in a field in the parish of Ellingham, fifty yards NE along the boundary fence with the North Sunderland road measured from the centre of the level crossing of the NER, then passing through or into the townships

The North Sunderland Railway Company.

(Incorporated by Act of Parliament, 55 and 56 Victoria, ch. civ.)

CAPITAL **£21,000,**

In 2,100 Shares of £10 each

£1 per Share to be paid on Application ; £2 per Share on Allotment.

CALLS to be made as the works proceed. £2 per Share to be the greatest amount of a Call, and three months at least to be the interval between successive Calls.

The liability of Shareholders is limited to the amount of their subscriptions.

The Company has power under its Act, subject to the subscription of the prescribed proportion of capital, to pay out of capital during construction interest at the rate of £3 per cent. per annum upon the amount, from time to time, paid up on Shares.

Directors.

Rev. DIXON DIXON-BROWN, J.P., D.L., Unthank Hall, Haltwhistle (Chairman).

HUGH ANDREWS, Esq., J.P., Swarland Hall, Acklington.

W. A. WATSON ARMSTRONG, Esq., J.P., Cragside, Rothbury.

Colonel ANTHONY MARSHALL, Annstead, North Sunderland.

J. D. MILBURN, Esq., J.P., ~~Barnhill, Newcastle-on-Tyne.~~ *Guyzance, Acklington*

Bankers.

Engineers.

R. ELLIOTT COOPER, Esq., M. Inst. C.E., 8, The Sanctuary, Westminster, London.

Solicitors.

Messrs. LEADBITTER & HARVEY, 57, Westgate Road, Newcastle-upon-Tyne.

Secretary and Offices.

RICH^D. SMITH, F.S.A.A., Clayton Chambers, 61, Westgate Road, Newcastle-upon-Tyne.

PROSPECTUS.

The North Sunderland Railway commences, as shewn by the accompanying map of the district, by a Junction with the North-Eastern Railway, at Chathill, and terminates at Seahouses, opposite the Lifeboat House.

It passes close to Fleetham, where it is intended to make a siding for agricultural purposes, and also to North Sunderland, where a small passenger station will be provided

Its total length is a little over four miles, and the railway will be a single line.

The need of a railway from Chathill to Seahouses has been felt since the construction of the Fishing Harbour (shewn on the accompanying plan) by Lord Crewe's Trustees, and will be increasingly felt in the event of the harbour being improved.

The want of such a means of access to this beautiful part of the Northumberland coast has prevented its great natural attractions from being available to the general public, and has also retarded the development of the district for business and residential purposes.

The railway will afford the means of working the coal, limestone, whinstone, fire-clay, and building stone deposits at and around North Sunderland and Seahouses, and it will give such facilities for the transit of fish and other materials from and to the harbour as will, it is expected, result in a large increase of business at Seahouses and North Sunderland.

One of the chief sources of traffic for the new line will, no doubt, be the fish traffic.

According to the Harbour Master's returns, the quantity of fish of all kinds landed at Seahouses is annually very considerable ; and there can be no question that the facilities that will be afforded by both harbour and railway for landing and despatching fish from Seahouses will increase, and attract a large portion of the fishing trade of the coast to this point, as the most convenient one from which this business can be carried on.

From information supplied by the North-Eastern Railway Company, the quantity of kippered and pickled herrings, white fish and shell fish (the great bulk of which was carted to the railway from Seahouses), manufactured fish manure, fish refuse, and refuse salt, despatched from Chathill Station was as follows :—

	1892.	1893.	1894.
(1.) Kippered and Pickled Herrings, White and Shell Fish ... ... Tons...	1,108	1,063	1,065
Manufactured Fish Manure ,, ...	195	286	300
Fish Refuse and Refuse Salt ,, ...	282	256	203
(2.) The Goods Traffic at Chathill Station, exclusive of the above, which was consigned to or received from persons at Seahouses and North Sunderland ... ... Tons...	1,775	1,532	1,193
(3.) The Coal Traffic received at Chathill Station, the bulk of which would be consumed in the district reached by the new line · ... ... Tons...	3,087	3,081	2,681
(4.) The Live Stock Traffic to and from Chathill Station, one-half of which at least would come from the district to be served by the new railway...Head	10,284	10,620	10,843

Although the total authorised Share and Loan Capital is £28,000, the Directors hope to construct and equip the line for a lesser sum ; and, in fact, they have had an offer from a competent contractor to construct the line for £18,000. The Charity Commissioners have assented to the Trustees of the late Lord Crewe taking Ordinary Shares in the proposed Railway to the extent of the agricultural value of the land to be acquired by the Company.

The picturesque features and historic associations of the district around Sea-houses, North Sunderland, and the coast, embracing as it does the Farne Islands, Holy Island, and Bamburgh, must, with the facilities for reaching them which the new line will afford, inevitably attract a large visitor and excursion traffic during the summer months, which, combined with the passenger and goods traffic arising from the fishing trade and incident to the resident population of the district, and the other sources of revenue from the working of the minerals in the district, mails, parcels, advertisements, &c., may be estimated to produce a substantial and increasing return per annum.

It is well known that coal, limestone, whinstone, building stone, and fire-clay exist in and around North Sunderland, and the development of those minerals may be expected to provide an additional traffic for the new railway.

From what has been previously stated as to the existing fish, goods, cattle, and coal traffic to and from Seahouses and North Sunderland, with no railway facilities whatever between Chathill and those places—a distance of five miles—it is anticipated that the construction of the proposed railway will result in this traffic being greatly increased.

The construction of the railway is almost certain to result in the improvement and deepening of the exhisting harbour at Seahouses (recently enlarged at great cost by Lord Crewe's Trustees), and its probable development into a port for shipment of such articles as whinstone for road metalling, bricks, limestone, and other products of the district, much of which would provide traffic for the new railway.

Lord Armstrong, who has recently acquired Bamburgh Castle estates, including the outer Farnes, has promised to take a substantial interest in the railway, which his Lordship and the Directors, in course of time, purpose to extend to Bamburgh, in the event of Parliamentary powers being obtained ; for, notwithstanding its difficulty of access, Bamburgh is already largely visited as a pleasure resort.

It is felt that the increasing tendency for business people to reside at seaside places during the summer months, and the great dearth of such resorts on the North-umberland coast, renders it desirable to speedily open up the district and to generally develop this attractive neighbourhood.

Applications for Shares, on the accompanying form, may be forwarded, with the amount payable, on application to the Company's Bankers, at Newcastle-upon-Tyne, or any of their branches.

Forms of application for Shares, and copies of this Prospectus, can be obtained at the offices either of the Company, or its Bankers, or Solicitors.

In cases where the number of Shares allotted is fewer than that asked for, the balance of the deposit will be applied towards the amount due on allotment, and any excess will be returned to the applicant. In cases where no allotment is made the deposit will be returned in full.

NORTH SUNDERLAND RAILWAY.

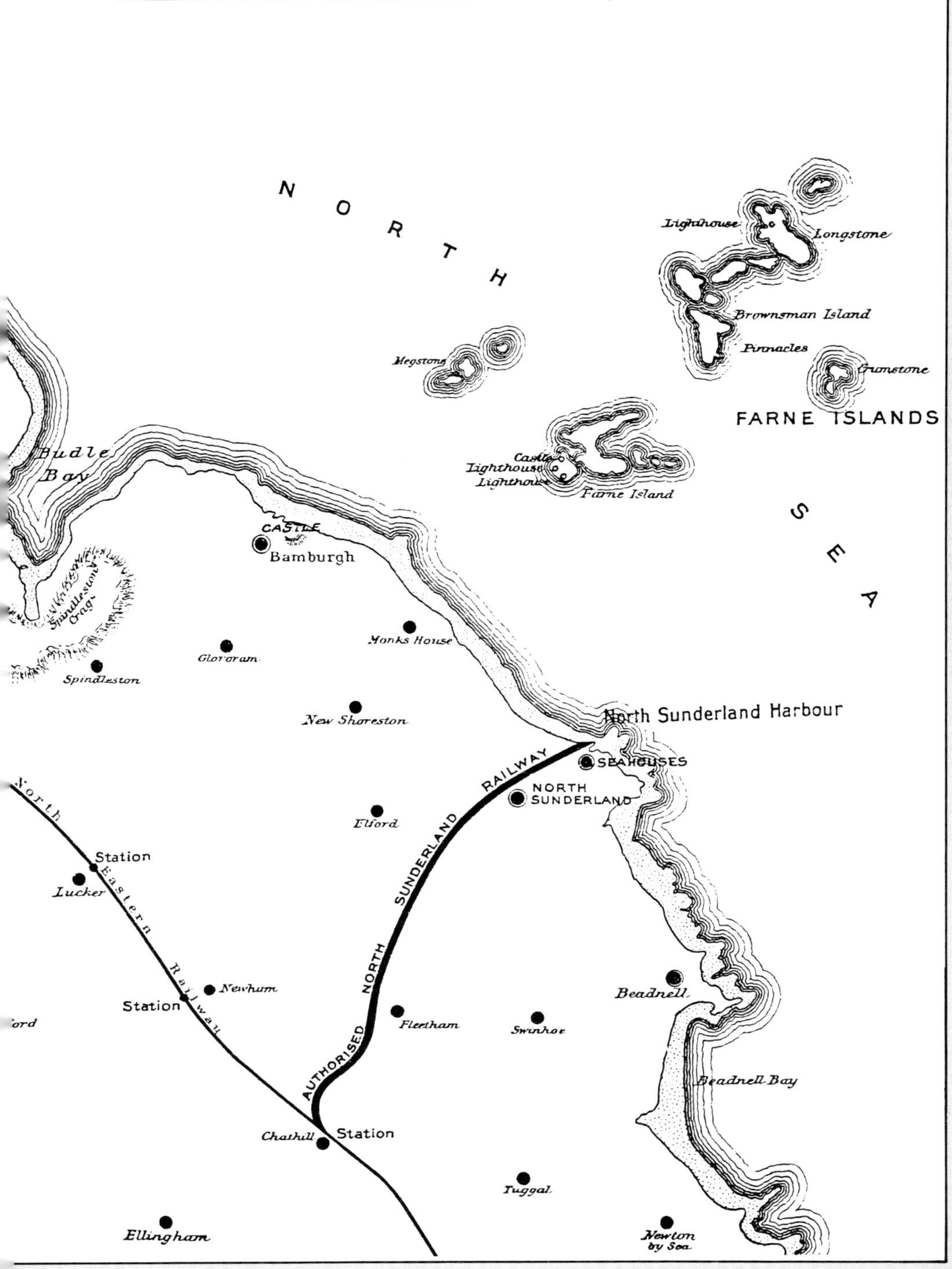

N O R T H

Lighthouse
Longstone

Brownsman Island

Pinnacles

Megstone

Gunstone

FARNE ISLANDS

Budle
Bay

Castle
Lighthouse
Lighthouse
Farne Island

S E A

CASTLE
Bamburgh

Spindleston Craig.

Monks House

Glororam

Spindleston

New Shoreston

North Sunderland Harbour

RAILWAY

SEAHOUSES

NORTH
SUNDERLAND

North
Eastern
Railway

Station

Lucker

Elford

AUTHORISED NORTH SUNDERLAND

Station

Newham

Fleetham

Swinhoe

Beadnell

ord

Beadnell Bay

Chathill
Station

Tuggal

Ellingham

Newton
by Sea

and places of Ellingham, Fleetham, Bamburgh, Swinhoe, North Sunderland, Seahouses and terminating in a field in the Parish of Bamburgh some twenty yards west of the lifeboat house at Seahouses.

2 A railway three furlongs one chain long commencing in the Parish of Ellingham and terminating in the Parish of Bamburgh by a junction with the intended railway No. 1.

The junction with the NER was to be at such a point within the limits of deviation shown in the plans and to be executed in such a manner as was reasonably required by the NER Engineer. Such connections were to be maintained by the Company as required by him for the proper accommodation of the traffic passing over the junction.

The authorised capital of the NSR was £21,000 made up from 2100 shares at £10 each. Borrowing powers were limited to £7000 and the number of Directors was fixed at a maximum of five and a minimum of three, three Directors to form a quorum. To be a Director a person had to hold 20 shares in his own right. The plans and specifications were drawn up by the same Newcastle consulting engineers used by Lord Crewe's trustees for their harbour works.

In 1898 a Light Railway Order was obtained by the NSR which authorised the construction of an extension towards Bamburgh and the operation of the original railway as a light railway. In spite of this Order the title of the Company remained unchanged.

Under this Order the North Sunderland Railway was allowed to raise a further £10,000 capital, of which £9920 was issued, made up of 992 preference shares of £10 each. This capital was allowed to be used to meet the requirements of the railway being built under the 1892 Act.

Construction and operation of the railway under the Order meant that passenger carrying trains need not be provided with continuous brakes as long as all trains had sufficient brake power, either manually or automatically applied, for the stoppage of any portion which might break away. Platforms need not be provided so long as all passenger coaches on the line were constructed so that their lowest footboard was not more than 16 inches above ground level. Any platform provided was to be no lower than 16 inches below the lowest coach footboard. No obligation existed for the company to provide shelter or conveniences at any station or stopping point. Rails used were to weigh not less than 60 pounds per yard, and on curves less than 9 chains radius they were to be tied to gauge by iron or steel ties suitably spaced and a check rail was to be provided. If the rails were flat bottomed and the sleepers wooden the rails were to be secured to the sleepers at joints by fang or other through bolts, or by coach screws or double spikes on the outside of the rails. Turntables need not be provided but any tender engines in use were not to run tender first at any time faster than 15 mph. Signals need not be interlocked with points.

No train or engine on the railway was to run at a speed exceeding 25 mph, or exceeding 10 mph when passing round a curve less than nine chains radius, or passing over any facing points not interlocked with a fixed or permanent semaphore signal and automatically fastened in a manner approved by the Board of Trade. The NSR was to erect and maintain at all times gates across the railway at each side of the road at level crossings. Unless permitted by the Board of Trade in writing the NSR was to employ a proper person to open and close the gates which were to be kept closed across the railway except during the time a train was crossing the road. The gates were to be of such size and dimensions and constructed so that when closed the railway would be fenced in to prevent cattle and horses from entering upon the railway. The drivers or conductors of trains passing along the railway line were to close the gates as soon as the train had passed. All lines of railway across roads were to be single track.

According to a note in *The Locomotive*, April 1900, it was stated by an NSR official that the railway was one of the first, if not the first, to be built under the Light Railways Act of 1896.

The North Sunderland Railway now had its empowering Act, later its Light Railway Order. All that was needed was the capital to construct it!

NORTH SUNDERLAND RAILWAY   B1571/9

C. N. MONTAGUE   SECRETARY & ACCOUNTANT'S OFFICE
Secretary & Accountant   CENTRAL STATION
Telephone   NEWCASTLE-UPON-TYNE
NEWCASTLE 21579

Letterhead design of the NSR, when under LNER/BR control.

Chapter Two
Construction

Having obtained the Act of Parliament the Directors first met at 144 Northumberland Street, Newcastle-on-Tyne on 21st March, 1893, to hear a proposal from Messrs Sharpe & Co., Contractors, of Leytonstone, Essex, who were prepared to build the railway complete for the share and loan capital less £1000, they taking £13,000 in fully paid shares. The Directors resolved not to consider the proposal but decided to make an effort and raise the capital privately by issuing a prospectus. The Board were not able to agree on the style of this prospectus, and at various times added details of fish traffic via Chathill and particulars of Seahouses harbour. Sharpes remained keen on building the NSR and in July they placed a further proposal before the Board who were still against the offer.

By August a list of 400 applications for shares was compiled. In that month Mr Sharpe met the Directors and offered to go ahead with the line for £16,150 cash, or he would accept £5000 cash and the handing over to him of £7000 worth of debentures and the rest of the contract price in fully paid up shares. This time the NSR Board showed some interest and asked for more particulars of the offer so they could go to the Board of Trade. Meanwhile it was decided to contact the Yorkshire Trust Ltd. of Leeds to see if they were interested in financing the line as it was understood this concern was interested in deepening the harbour. Sharpes put their offer in writing but on 25th September the Directors learned that the Yorkshire Trust was not prepared to finance the line. After discussing Mr Sharpe's offer the Board decided not to accept it.

Still looking for ways of financing the undertaking the Board met on 2nd February, 1894 to discuss an offer from another firm of contractors, Messrs Pearsons, who were prepared to carry out the work including provision of permanent way, buildings, three passenger coaches and one locomotive for £20,500. They would complete the work within twelve months providing they could get immediate possession of the land. It was necessary for the Directors to defer a decision on the offer and in March, Pearsons were told that negotiations were still in progress.

Another contender for the contract came on the scene in April, Philips of Brechin, whose proposals the Board felt were very reasonable, so reasonable in fact that the Directors said that, subject to the confirmation of another meeting, they would be prepared to negotiate. Meanwhile a proposal was received from Carlton Hessey & Co. in July. This proposal was deferred and the Board decided to once more negotiate with Sharpe who had again contacted them. In Sep-

A panoramic view of Seahouses station and yard. *Bamburgh* and the two ex-North Eastern coaches are on view in this mid-twenties scene.

Author's Collection

With No. 68089 (cab leading) at its head, the afternoon train is ready to leave Seahouses station. There cannot have been a big fish auction, as there is only one fish van on the train. The postman has just brought the mailbags from the post office on his barrow, for the train.

N. Stead Collection

A panoramic view of Seahouses Station shortly after opening of the railway. Locomotive *Bamburgh* shunts in the goods yard. The ex-Highland coaches wait in the platform. The engine shed with round roof and the full width glazing in the warehouse are clearly visible.

Northumberland County Records Office

Bamburgh at Seahouses, August 1921. NER coaches form the train with NER fish wagons and van between the locomotive and the coaches. Note ground signal remains and the trap point blades. *Author's Collection*

The Lady Armstrong at the head of the morning mixed train, again with unbraked wagons between the locomotive and coach seen here at Seahouses station in June 1938. *W.H. Tate*

Bamburgh and the three ex-NER coaches at Seahouses station. Note the warehouse end-wall windows.   *Author's Collection*

No. 68089 leaves Seahouses in September 1951. Although only a few weeks from closure, the locomotive is beautifully turned out.   *Author's Collection*

Class 'Y7' No. 68089 ready to leave Chathill in September 1950. There is a typical NER oil lamp near the locomotive. The ground frame cabin can be seen on the middle-left.
Author's Collection

Lower quadrant signals are prominent as the diesel propels an ex-NER auto-coach trailer into the bay at Chathill (this was on loan to the NSR). The coach would not be used as a control trailer, because the locomotive did not have the necessary auto-gear fitted.
H.N. James

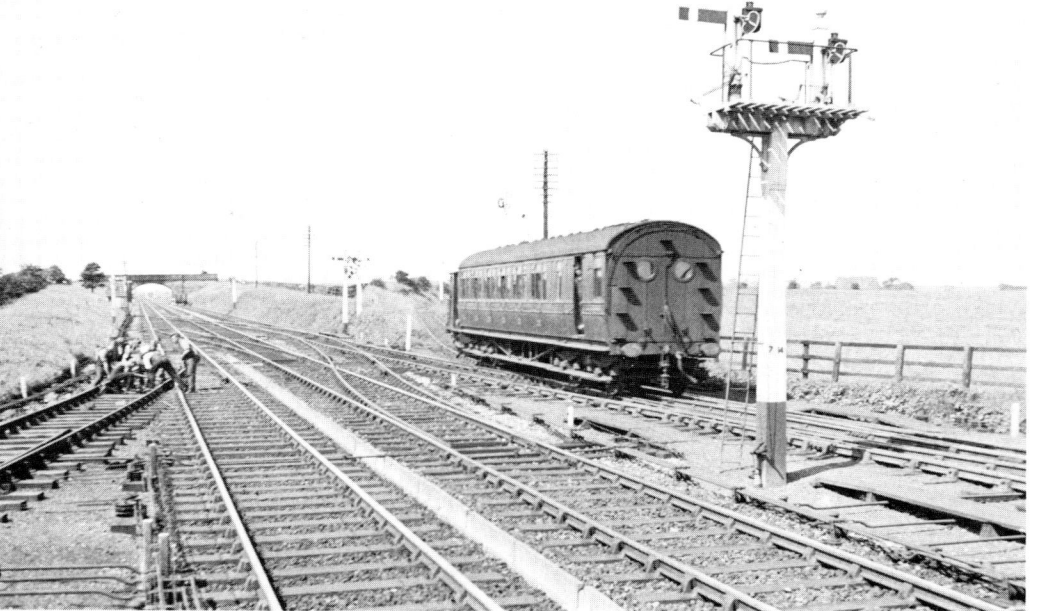

The diesel locomotive shunting at Chathill. *Author's Collection*

Locomotive *Bamburgh* ready to leave Chathill in April 1923 at the head of the railway's two coaches and van. *Ken Nunn*

NER No. 407 and the three ex-NER coaches approaching Chathill Cutting.

C.L.J. Romanes

NER No. 407 and the two NER coaches of the time leave Seahouses for Chathill on 24th May, 1919. The catch point and ground signal can be seen, proof that this line was not a "light railway". *Ken Nunn*

Class 'Y7' simmering in the shed at Seahouses. This view shows the shed construction well. *Author*

Seahouses station. The NSR's ex-NER and one GER coach plus a BR fish van wait in the platform for the 'Y7' (lurking in the shed) to return. *Author*

tember it was learned that the latter could not find a financier and so all negotiations with him came to an end. Philips, after going over the route of the railway laid a proposal before the Board as follows:

> The contract sum to be £18,000 on condition that the work was split into two and work on the second portion was not to start until the NSR Directors had given an assurance that they had the cash to pay for the same. With that consideration in mind he was prepared to take a third of the first payment division, i.e. £10,000 in fully paid up shares. The division of the work was to be: first part – fencing, level crossing gates, accommo-dation work, bridges, approaches, culverts and earthworks. The second part covered the provision of the permanent way and ballast, stations and gatehouses, sidings, signals and twelve months' guaranteed maintenance, and he undertook to begin the works and supply all the necessary plant on receipt of a letter saying he could take possession of the land.

As the Board had still not got the necessary finance they had to defer a decision on this offer.

Eighteen months had now gone by since the first Directors' meet-ing and they were still no further forward with their railway – in fact they had not even got the necessary financial backing. Therefore it must have been welcome news to them when the Board met on 5th November, 1894, that Lord Armstrong was prepared to subscribe and become a Director. Throughout the early life of the company Direc-tors came and went, no doubt the uncertainty of the undertaking had a bearing on this. Lord Armstrong, whose Bamburgh Castle was three miles north of Seahouses, was strongly in favour of an exten-sion of the NSR to Bamburgh and also the deepening of the harbour at Seahouses. On this occasion a map and estimate of cost of the extension was produced, the cost being estimated at £15,000.

Mr Philips must have been sure of his chances of winning the contract as on 5th November Mr Ewing, one of the Board, asked on whose authority the line had been staked out and borings taken. The Secretary was asked to write to Philips in confirmation of his son's statement that any work done and costs incurred would be his own responsibility.

The first ray of hope in the Directors' search for finance came on 26th February, 1895 when a letter from the Reverend Dixon Dixon-Brown, Chairman of the Board, was read. In this he said that a certain friend of his had influential friends who were prepared to practically support the whole undertaking on conditions which would necessi-tate certain alterations in the management of the company. They required a new Board of Directors to be set up consisting as far as possible of local people so giving confidence to people in the neigh-bourhood. A new firm of solicitors was also required. The Directors discussed this seemingly fortuitous turn of events and decided to issue a new prospectus setting forth the contemplated changes in management and making mention of Lord Armstrong's support.

Events started to move at last and in March it was decided to bring in Messrs J. Wyatt Sanderson and Moncrieff as engineers, to act along with the company's Engineer, Mr Elliott Cooper. The search for backers continued and the Directors decided to advertise the new prospectus in various local papers to test public reaction. The Company's Parliamentary agents were approached to see if it was possible to increase the number of Directors and to find out the Company's legal position if the powers of construction ran out. The agents told the Board that to increase their number would require a further Act of Parliament but that the extinguishing of the powers would not make much difference.

Whilst enamoured with Mr Dixon Dixon-Brown's proposal the Directors were still in touch with Philips who, in July, said he was prepared to accept shares instead of cash.

October came, and still no decisions had been taken on Philips' offer; the Board approached him to see if he was open to modifications in his offer. The revised prospectus, with an insertion giving details of the 1895 fish landings at Seahouses and a reference to golf links at Bamburgh, was approved, along with a map of the railway and harbour at Seahouses. The repeated connection of the railway and harbour is of interest, one of the many schemes proposed for extending and improving the harbour included a railway station at the place now occupied by the lifeboat house.

Finally in December 1895 a Mr Kite, the friend of Rev. Dixon Dixon-Brown, presented a proposal to the Directors on which they looked favourably. Mr Kite was informed that after his contractors had been over the ground and met them they could enter into a provisional contract. Consequently the Board met on 18th December, 1895; the Directors were reminded that their powers of compulsory purchase had expired on 27th June of that year but that the landowners were prepared to ignore this fact. Mr Kite was invited to bring in his friends, Mr A. Haslett, Contractor; Mr G. Levick, Engineer; and Mr T. Griesbach of Hansworth, Birmingham, the Financier, to confirm their offer as follows:

> For the construction of the railway and its equipment – £20,000, purchase of land – £2500, administration charges – £1500, making a total of £24,000. The contractor could take part payment of £10,000 in ordinary shares and allow 10 per cent rebate to the company on those shares subscribed for by the public. The contractor was to deposit with the Company, on signing the contract, £1000 to be released on four equal payments on Engineers' certificates for work done, viz £250 for one quarter of the work and so on to completion. The contractor was to be paid £500 in cash against an Engin-

eer's certificate in respect of plant and machinery placed on the ground. The contractor was to be paid for work done against Engineer's certificates in cash and shares in equal proportions.

Haslett and his friends were told that this offer was very favourable and the Company's solicitor was instructed to ask Howlett's solicitor to prepare a provisional contract in time for the next Board meeting. At the same time enquiries would be made of the Company's Engineer asking if it was usual to pay cash against plant and the Directors would investigate Haslett's financial standing. At the end of December, when the Directors next met, they decided to defer the provisional contract until they had obtained satisfactory references for Haslett and they also wished his contractor to be a party to the contract. When this was satisfactorily agreed between both parties the prospectus would be issued. On the last day of 1895 the Directors were prepared to enter into the provisional contract with Haslett, reserving the right to withdraw if public feeling towards the undertaking was not satisfactory. By 3rd January, 1896 the draft of the provisional contract was put before the Board, but, as several clauses including the withdrawal clause had to be added, they took no action. It was decided to pay interest on capital already invested in the Company.

Everything pointed to the railway now being built with only small details to be settled before the contract was signed. However, at the end of January the Board were told that in spite of the contractor's solicitor being told of the necessity of the withdrawal clause it had still not been written into the contract. They therefore resolved to proceed no further with the matter and abandon all negotiations.

The scene was not so rosy on 17th March, 1896 when the Directors finally realised that, as the shares were not going very well, the whole railway undertaking might have to be abandoned. On that day a further proposal was received from Philips and the Board decided to write to him and Kite informing them that they were having difficulty raising capital and asking would they be prepared to make further proposals under the circumstances.

Haslett and his friends who were present proposed that the contract price be £24,500, an increase of £500 over their earlier proposal, of which £9000 was to be in cash, £7000 in debentures or cash and shares of £8500. In considering the offer the Directors suggested that subscribers be asked whether or not the proposed railway should be built taking into consideration its probable cost, the amount of capital subscribed, and the proposed means of raising money. This question was answered in May, when it was revealed that on the first issue of the prospectus some 670 applications had been received, and on the second issue, 300. A memorial from Seahouses was received bearing

203 signatures asking the Directors to proceed with the construction of the line. A letter from Haslett was read in which he agreed to limit his voting rights to one-eighth of his holding and, after discussion, it was agreed to draw up a final contract for building the railway. It was decided to allot the shares and the call was to be payable on or before 13th May, 1896 – not quite three years and two months after the first Board meeting.

By July things were moving again and the decision was taken to place the Common Seal of the Company on the contract in the presence of the Chairman and Secretary at such a date as they may be advised by their solicitor. It was agreed to pay Haslett the full £500 for plant and machinery on receipt of his £1000 deposit and Colonel Marshall, one of the Directors, was asked to see the Duke of North-umberland's Commissioner with a view to the abandoning of the proposed station at Fleetham in an attempt to reduce costs. However, in September the non-completion of the contract was discussed by the Board and Haslett, the latter having intimated that he was not in the position to deposit £1000 with the Company on the signing of the contract. The Directors decided to seek Counsel's opinion with a view to ascertaining the Company's position and adopt such a course advised in the interests of the shareholders. A letter was sent to Haslett telling him that unless £1000 was paid by a given date they would proceed no further and consider all arrangements at an end. A reply from Haslett stated that the deposit would not be forthcoming, therefore the Directors decided that as he had failed to fulfil the primary conditions of the contract they must decline to proceed any further and instructed their solicitor to terminate all negotiations with Haslett to protect the interests of the Company. The Company's Engineers were to go to Seahouses at an early date to take measure of the work done by Haslett and take stock of the plant in use.

No time was lost and on 10th October the Engineers gave their report in which a total value of materials of £1120 was given. Haslett's account had been received claiming £2266 10s. 11d. The report stated that work had been started on the railway. Certain earthworks had been commenced along with a limited amount of fencing. A short length of standard gauge track had been laid at the Chathill end of the line whereon was a four-wheeled trolley. At Seahouses there was a stock of light section rail and some 3 ft gauge tipping wagons whilst an old mill at North Sunderland had been adapted to serve as labour-ers' barracks. All work was at a standstill. On this occasion a letter from Mr Meyer of Leeds was read offering to construct the railway but consideration was deferred until a proper estimate was received.

On 12th October, 1896 a further letter from Meyer was read to the Directors together with specifications and plans from Whitaker Bros,

Contractors, of Leeds. Meyer was prepared to obtain contracts for the whole work between Chathill and Seahouses including the junction with the NER for £19,000. There could perhaps be a saving to the Company when he was in receipt of full plans. This figure covered the whole railway in working order but the locomotive and rolling stock would have to be on the hire system over seven years. The contractors were to be paid partially in cash and partially in bonds. Meyer felt that the Company would need £2000 for administration charges and to settle with Haslett. On the whole some £21,000 would be required of which £8000 was already subscribed. The sum of money could be raised thus – shares, £8000; debenture stock £7000 and rent charges on premiums or debentures, £6000, making a total of £21,000. Meyer concluded his letter by saying that he presumed that having regard to the position of the Company, the Directors would insist upon rigid economy in the works to be executed.

After discussion, the Directors decided that the construction of the railway on the lines suggested by Meyer be accepted subject to the preparation of the contract with the usual proper clauses to be approved by the Directors. They also decided to make a call of £2 per share.

At last it now seemed as though the railway would be built after all the tribulations of the past three and a half years. At the Board meeting at the end of October a draft of the contract between the NSR and Whitakers was submitted, and, after discussion, it was arranged that the two parties' solicitors meet and prepare the final contract. The Haslett business was not settled however, as it was reported that once more Counsel's advice had been sought and it was thought to be favourable to the Company.

By 4th November construction was well under way and negotiations had opened with the NER over a temporary connection to facilitate transfer of materials. On 13th November, 1896 the Company's seal was put on the contract with Whitakers.

The settlement with Haslett was a protracted affair and when a Board meeting was held in the last week of 1896 his account was considered. Owing to its excessiveness they unanimously declined to accept it and expressed their willingness to refer the matter to an independent engineer to be appointed by Sir Benjamin Baker CE, President of the Civil Engineers, or the Board of Trade.

In May 1897 the Directors inspected the works and in that month, when the first Engineer's certificate was presented, the first payment to him was made. A further call of £2 per share was made that month.

The Light Railways Act had been passed in 1896 and in July 1897 Meyer suggested to the Board that by applying for an Order, they could possibly make considerable savings by the simplifications to stations and signals that would be allowed. Whilst very keen on this idea the Board sought more information on the proposed savings before they considered the idea in full. It was also suggested that a proposed extension to Monks House be covered by the Light Railway Order application. (This was the extension towards Bamburgh which Lord Armstrong favoured.) Later in the month the decision was taken to go ahead with the application, estimated costs of £3000 per mile were given for the extension.

A final call of £1 per share was made on 17th September, 1897. Of the authorised capital for the railway and the extension the following was issued: £14,900, of which 930 £10 shares were issued for cash and 560 fully paid up shares were issued in consideration of land etc. Most of the cash shares were taken up by the local people who stood to gain from the building of the line. The shares were never quoted on the Stock Exchange. Under the Light Railway Order a further capital of £10,000 was allowed of which £9920 was issued, consisting of 992 preference shares of £10 each.

In July negotiations started with the North Eastern Railway regarding the North Sunderland Railway being built from the temporary junction so calling for a change of plans on their part. The draft for the Light Railway Order was approved in November at a special general meeting of the Company and submitted to the Company's Parliamentary agents. As recorded in *Chapter 1*, this order was granted in 1898.

Matters with Haslett had still not been settled by December 1897 and an offer made to him by the Board was refused. Meanwhile, struggling for his money, he took action against the NSR through the Court of the Queen's Bench and on 22nd March, 1898 the Board learned that the Court's decision had gone in favour of Haslett and he had also been awarded costs. The NSR paid up and so ended the Haslett affair.

Negotiations with the North Eastern Railway over the Chathill layout continued and the eventual outcome was to make use of that railway's bay platform instead of a separate station so saving the North Sunderland Railway a considerable sum.

As the Company had to pay Haslett more money than expected rent charges were raised on the land over which the railway ran to help finances. These negotiations were arranged by Mr Meyer who had also purchased the land for the railway taking shares to the value thereof.

Hire purchase arrangements were made with the Yorkshire Wagon Co. Ltd in June 1898 regarding the purchase of the locomotive over seven years. Coaching stock was purchased second-hand from the Highland Railway and arrangements made with the NER for the loan of wagons. On 1st August, 1898 the railway was in business for goods traffic. On 5th October the official Board of Trade inspection was carried out. Following the Inspector's report certain works had to be carried out before passenger carrying began on 18th December, 1898, five years and nine months after the first Directors' meeting.

Chapter Three
The Route described

In spite of a letter from the Engineer of the North Eastern Railway advising the Directors of the NSR that, if NER locomotives were to work over their line it would have to be laid with 82 lb. rails supported in 40 lb. chairs, the railway was laid with 63 lb. flat bottom rail spiked direct to the wooden sleepers. In the 1940s, under LNER auspices, parts of the line were relaid on concrete pot sleepers. Certain sections were later relaid on wooden sleepers but the concrete type were still in use when the railway closed.

The original proposal was for the North Sunderland Railway to have its own single-faced terminus platform at Chathill in the field behind the North Eastern Railway warehouse, then to pass through a run-round loop and over a connection with the NER warehouse road and into a cutting. When the line was being constructed a temporary connection was installed by the NER corresponding more or less with the proposed railway No. 2 and the cutting was excavated from this point. To save the cost of a separate station it was eventually agreed with the NER management that use be made of a bay platform constructed at the back of the up platform at Chathill, and it is from there that the railway eventually commenced. Exit from the platform was controlled by signals from Chathill signal box at the south end of the down platform; signals were necessary because the NSR train had to cross the NER connections to their goods yard by means of a double slip point.

In the cutting the change of rail section marked the start of the NSR metals. With the main line signal standing on the left flank like a sentinel, the line went deeper into the cutting before swinging right on a ten chain curve through approximately 90 degrees and emerged on tangent track over an occupation crossing. This crossing over an intake or drove was always treated by the NSR as a farm crossing although the Act required them to consider it as a level crossing over

a public road. Carrying straight on the line crossed a low embankment, then on a plate girder bridge with concrete abutments, it went
over the Long Nanny Burn. Between the crossing and the bridge a
run-round loop was laid on the left side, the points were controlled
by a small ground frame at the Chathill end. Near the burn and on the
left side of the track stood a cylindrical water tank on three yellow
brick piers; the tank had seen previous service elsewhere as a Lanca-
shire boiler.

This water tank was something of a landmark and was referred to
as a feature of interest in the LNER's pre-war East Coast guide book
(provided free for passengers) "On Either Side". The Seahouses
water was very hard in 1898 hence the need for the tank. Although it
cannot be confirmed, the most likely original pump installation was
hand operated by means of a large flywheel. Later, using a steam
pump mounted on the locomotive, the water could be pumped from
the burn to the storage tank easily then the locomotive saddle tank
could be filled as required. In 1920 a new supply of water was
available at Seahouses and the tank fell out of use. When the diesel
locomotive was obtained it was proposed to convert it to store diesel
fuel oil, but so little fuel was used by the locomotive that the usual
method of supply was from drums stored in Seahouses shed.

The light construction of the Long Nanny Bridge was one of the
reasons for the imposition of axle load restrictions on the line which
led to difficulties in later years when relief motive power was sought.
From the burn the line ran across a low embankment then turned left
into a cutting and passed under the Fleetham–Elford road. The
bridge here had concrete abutments and plate girder sides. Through
the bridge the site of the proposed Fleetham station was passed,
then, with the line striking a dead straight course, the cutting was left
and an embankment reached before the Swinhoe Burn was crossed
on a culvert type of bridge. Shortly after passing over the burn a
connection from the quarry trailed in from the left.

The quarry, known as the Pasture Hill Quarry, was worked from
approximately 1907 to 1913. The connection and tracks beyond the
NSR boundary fence were removed long before the railway closed.
However, the points, controlled by a small ground frame on the
north side of the line, remained in place until closure.

Clearing the embankment the line ran into another cutting and,
climbing once more, breasted the summit alongside a farm cottage.
For its size the NSR had a considerable amount of earthworks. From
the summit, the line dropped gently through cuttings and over
embankments until it swung southwards and passed under the
Swinhoe–Shorestone Road. The railway was fenced throughout with
post-and-rail type fencing, small gates and stiles for farm workers'

Chathill for Seahouses Station in Northumberland taken in July 1962, showing the fine station building, footbridge and signal box. The North Sunderland Bay platform is on the left with the goods vans *in situ*.　　　　*A. Wood*

A view taken from the cab of *The Lady Armstrong,* portraying Chathill in 1936. The double catch point in front of the locomotive should be noticed as also the lower quadrant signals.　　　　*W.H. Tate*

The start of the railway at Chathill with the change of rail section easily noticeable. Beyond the gate (erected to show the BR boundary) is the junction signal for the Chathill station's Bay platform (*upper quadrant*) and the goods yard (*lower quadrant*). *Author*

Looking along the railway towards the Fleetham Bridge, from the "summit". *Author's Collection*

On the same day, rounding the curve towards the Long Nanny loop, the single upper quadrant signal protects Chathill station. *W.H. Tate*

Further around the curve, the wooden chocks to retain the rails to gauge can clearly be seen. *W.H. Tate*

The Long Nanny Burn water tank; a view looking towards Fleetham in November 1951. The fixed distant signal for Chathill can just be discerned.
Author's Collection

The Long Nanny Burn bridge seen here after closure (1964). A fence hangs from the handrail, its purpose was to stop cattle passing through. *Author*

The fixed distant signal with the water tower in the distance. In this view the concrete sleepers can be seen (November 1951). *Author*

The Fleetham Bridge seen from the cab of *The Lady Armstrong* as she approaches from Chathill in July 1938. *W.H. Tate*

Top
View up the incline towards Herds House (October 1951).
Author's Collection

Left
Pasture Hill bridge looking towards North Sunderland (October 1951).
Author's Collection

Below
Approaching North Sunderland station in July 1938, seen from the cab of *The Lady Armstrong*. The points to the "Long Siding" can be seen, also the grounded body of the NER birdcage coach.
W.H. Tate

North Sunderland platform, July 1938. The NER underframe is under the hammer. The diverted road required by the Justices can be picked out on the left. *W.H. Tate*

A view of North Sunderland station from the Shoreston road. The "corrugated gothic" station buildings are clearly visible. *Author's Collection*

North Sunderland platform in 1934, still oil lit. *Bamburgh* is in the station yard where it was overhauled. *H.C. Casserley*

The Lady Armstrong is nearly at Seahouses. The ground frame can be seen on the left but the ground signals have gone by this date in 1938.   *W.H. Tate*

Seahouses station and yard in 1938 seen from the diesel loco's cab. The extension to the engine shed, the modifications to the warehouse and the goods yard crane should be noticed.   *W.H. Tate*

Seahouses yard, looking from the platform towards the road. The path for passengers was on the left side. The engine shed is straight ahead and warehouse to the right. Note the mixed wood and concrete sleepers (May 1951). *Author's Collection*

Seahouses station buildings viewed from the road with the footpath on the right. The crossing over the track to the platform can also be seen (May 1951). *Author's Collection*

A close-up of the Seahouses station buildings (May 1951). *Author's Collection*

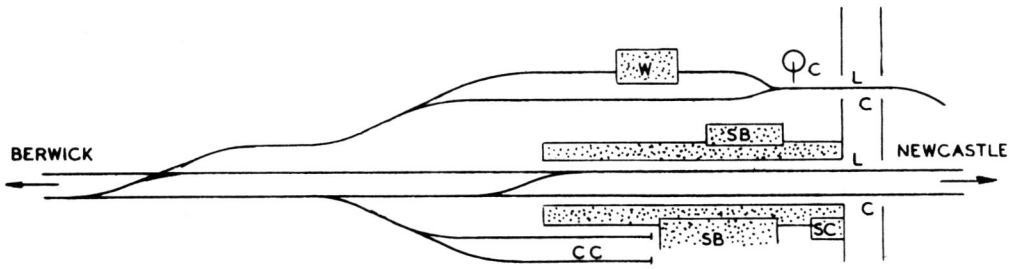

LAYOUT IN 1895

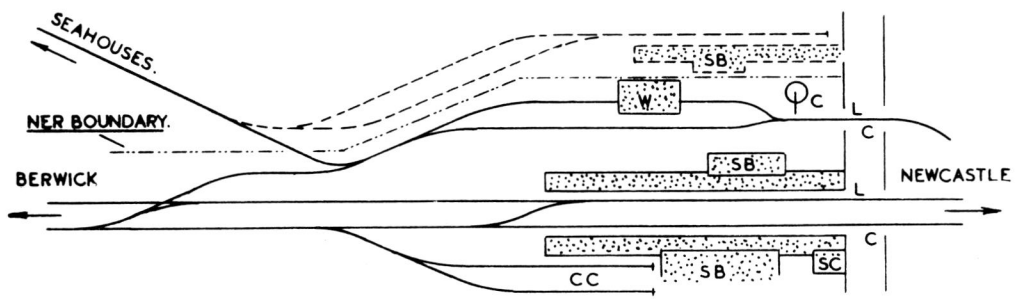

**TEMPORARY CONNECTION &
PROPOSED N.S.R.
TERMINUS.**

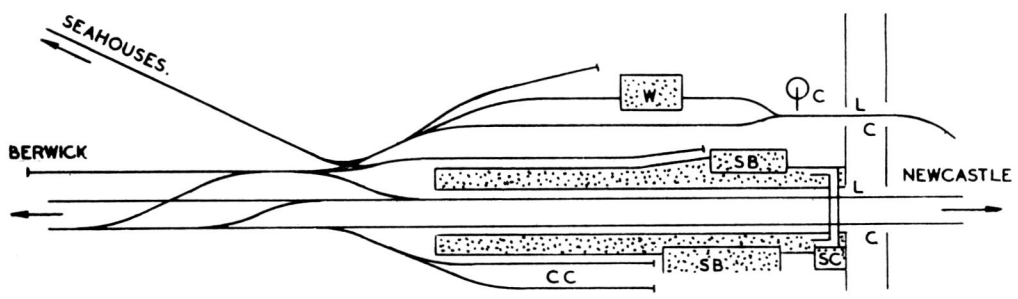

C	CRANE.
W	WAREHOUSE.
CC	COAL CELLS.
LC	LEVEL CROSSING.
SB	STATION BUILDINGS.
SC	SIGNAL CABIN.

FINAL LAYOUT.

Maps of Chathill station at various dates.

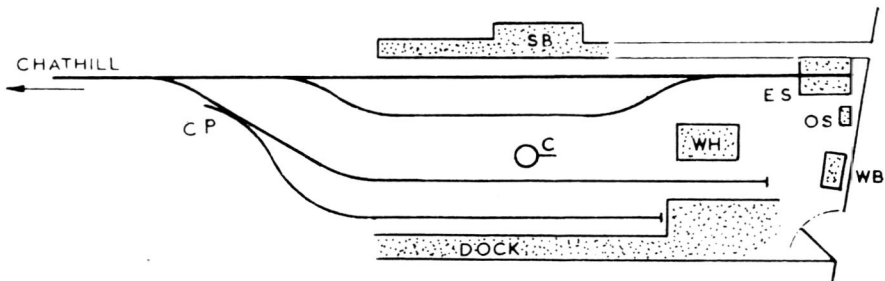

PROPOSED LAYOUT.

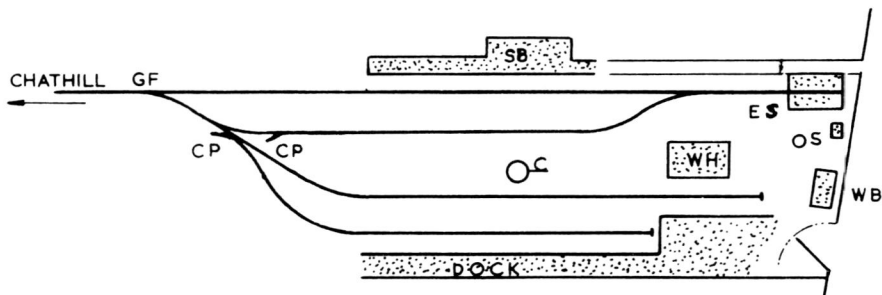

CHATHILL

SB

ES

OS

WH

C

WB

CP

DOCK

CHATHILL GF

SB

ES

OS

WH

C

WB

CP   CP

DOCK

C	CRANE.
CP	CATCH POINTS.
ES	ENGINE SHED.
GF	GROUND FRAME.
OS	OIL STORE.
SB	STATION BUILDINGS.
WB	WEIGHBRIDGE.
WH	WAREHOUSE.

ACTUAL LAYOUT.

Map of Seahouses station, proposed and final layouts.

use were marked along this section of the line by tall poles.

The second bridge was a skew structure, again with concrete abutments and steel plate girder sides. Emerging from the cutting the passengers got their first glimpse of the sea when to the south the expanse of Beadnell Bay could be seen. Crossing the Engine Inn Burn on a concrete culvert, the line passed once more into a cutting where another summit was encountered, the line then dropped to North Sunderland over an embankment.

At North Sunderland there was a siding on the north side connected to the main line by a trailing crossover. A passenger platform was provided and a corrugated iron building which was originally the station but was later converted to a house. The road from Shoreston to North Sunderland originally went straight across the line of the railway and under Section 33 of the 1892 Act the NSR was required to build a new section of road towards the Broad Road parallel to the line of the railway. Only when this piece of road was completed to the satisfaction of the Justices and opened for public use was the NSR allowed to close the old road and build their line across it, all rights of way ceasing. The level crossing over the Broad Road was protected by hand operated gates. Under the Light Railway Order the railway was relieved of the need to build a public footbridge over the line at this place.

Over the road, skirting a low hill with the land rising to the north, and then veering northwards the line passed the school on the right and entered a cutting before Seahouses station was approached. Between North Sunderland and Seahouses the line followed the road and gradually houses were built backing onto the railway.

Seahouses station was the headquarters of the railway although the Secretary had his office in Newcastle-upon-Tyne. The line entered the station with the platform and buildings on the left. A run-round loop was on the right as also were the two sidings, one of which served a lengthy fish dock, whilst the other, a public siding, served the coal pens, the crane and the warehouse. The railway ended a few yards from the Bamburgh road in an engine shed. The points at the North Sunderland end of the station were operated from a small ground frame on the north side of the track. Catch points were provided on the run-round loop and siding lead, ground signals were fitted to these points. The signals were removed but the catch points remained until the railway closed. The point at the shed end of the loop was worked by a local lever spring loaded for the loop.

Had it been built, the extension to Bamburgh would have trailed in from the north between North Sunderland station and the school.

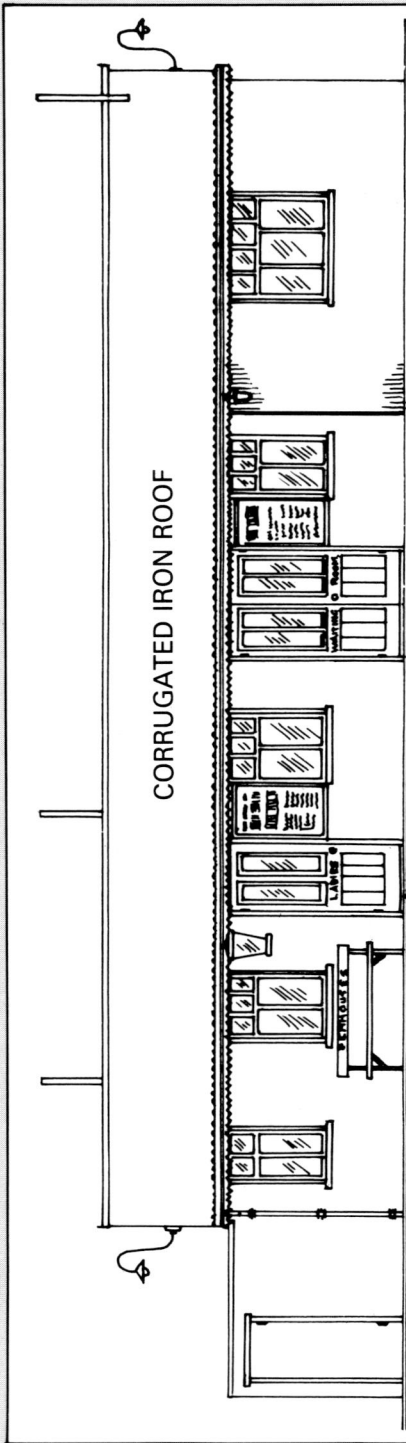

CORRUGATED IRON ROOF

STATION MASTER & BOOKING

WAITING ROOM, & PARCELS OFFICE

LADIES ROOM

LADIES WC

GENTS

Sketch of Seahouses Station buildings.

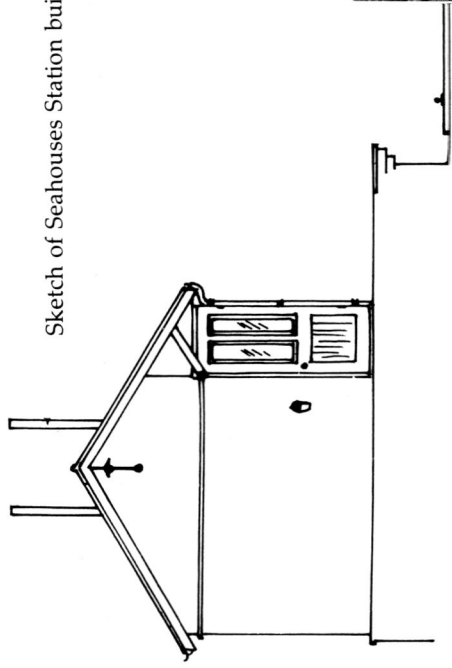

END ELEV^N (GENTS END)
OPPOSITE END, NO WINDOWS OR DOORS.

Chapter Four

The Station Buildings

All buildings on the railway were fabricated in corrugated iron and were supplied by David Rowell and Company, of London.

At Seahouses the station building was situated on the platform which was stone edged and surfaced with ash and macadam. The building had a peaked roof and consisted of the following offices from the road end – a station master's cum booking office, a general waiting room with ticket barrier, a ladies' room with lavatory and externally, a gentlemen's lavatory. The station master's office was the full width of the roof whilst the rest of the building was set back, the roof acting as a canopy. A garden on the platform was always well tended.

The engine shed was complete with an inspection pit and originally had a curved roof, in 1902 this was replaced by a peaked roof of slated construction. In 1934 the shed was extended with a semi-lean-to structure on the front so that both the NSR's locomotives could be kept under cover. A coal stage was built from sleepers outside the shed between the track and the station approach path.

Supported on wooden piles, the warehouse had sliding doors on both the rail and road sides; the curved roof provided a canopy over the railway and roadway so protecting goods during loading and unloading. The windows were set high up on the ends and in the early thirties were reduced in length. In the late forties the extent of the canopy overhang was reduced.

Just inside the goods yard gate was situated a weighbridge of ten tons capacity with a 12 ft by 6½ ft table supplied by Henry Pooley and Son. A peaked roof building housed the steelyard. Near the engine shed stood a curved roofed oil store which was sold in 1945 for £2.

Originally all buildings at Seahouses were oil-lit but in 1926 electric lighting was installed. In 1930 the Northumberland County Council were carrying out road widening at Seahouses and the station wall was set back and the weighhouse slightly altered.

Passengers approached the platform from the road by an ash path parallel to the railway, the gate was just to the Bamburgh side of the engine shed. A goods crane of two tons capacity was situated alongside the public road in the goods yard but in 1927, following a request from the NER for information, it was stated that the crane was unsafe and repairs were unlikely due to cost. As a result the reference to the crane was deleted from the NER Handbook of Stations. A crossing was made over the loop and platform road opposite the station master's office so that the road vehicles could back right up to the platform for easy trans-shipment of "smalls" traffic.

The fish dock was stone faced and had a ballast surface; coal pens were built from timber. In 1900 it was proposed to purchase more land to make the fish dock into an island platform and build a raised coal drop so allowing the use of NER bottom door wagons for land-sale coal traffic, but this never materialised.

North Sunderland station had buildings somewhat similar to those at Seahouses with a detached timber built platform. One of Mr Meyer's money-saving ideas was to convert the buildings into a dwelling for the guard whose wife would act as crossing keeper. In 1902 this was carried out. Following an accident to a female passenger in February 1925 it was proposed that a new platform be built as repairs to the timber one would be excessive and, on 16th November, 1925, the new brick built, stone edged, platform was brought into use.

A five ton weighbridge with a similar sized table to that at Sea-houses was installed in 1898 but in 1903 it was re-sold to the makers – Henry Pooley and Son.

Public access to the platform was by a wicket gate on the North Sunderland side of the crossing; a seat was provided under the canopy of the building for waiting passengers. The passenger plat-form did not have any cover for passengers. Originally oil lit, it was eventually provided with electric lights. The public siding was approached through a gate on the Bamburgh side of the level crossing.

At Chathill the North Eastern rebuilt the up platform and leng-thened it so providing a lengthy bay platform for the Seahouses train. The buffer end of this bay was used by the NSR to store spare rolling stock. The alterations to the station cost the NER £815 for permanent way and £1135 for signalling and interlocking, making a total of £1950. Mr Meyer met the NER authorities and managed to get the cost reduced to £1100. Payment to the NER was arranged at £44 per annum, with a £41 per annum rent charge for the platform and part of the wages of porters and signalmen. The waiting shed on the plat-form was rebuilt after the opening of the NSR. To meet the Board of Trade Inspector's requirements the North Eastern built a footbridge at the crossing end of the station. This was of the standard outline with elliptical arch but was fabricated from steel angles instead of the more usual cast iron sections. Chathill station was always oil-lit.

Passengers for the NSR trains obtained their tickets at the NER booking office on the down platform. Tickets issued from Chathill to North Sunderland stations were of North Eastern or its successor's usual type and carried their name. Tickets were issued for first, second, and third class fares and passengers waited for their trains on the up platform.

DOCK

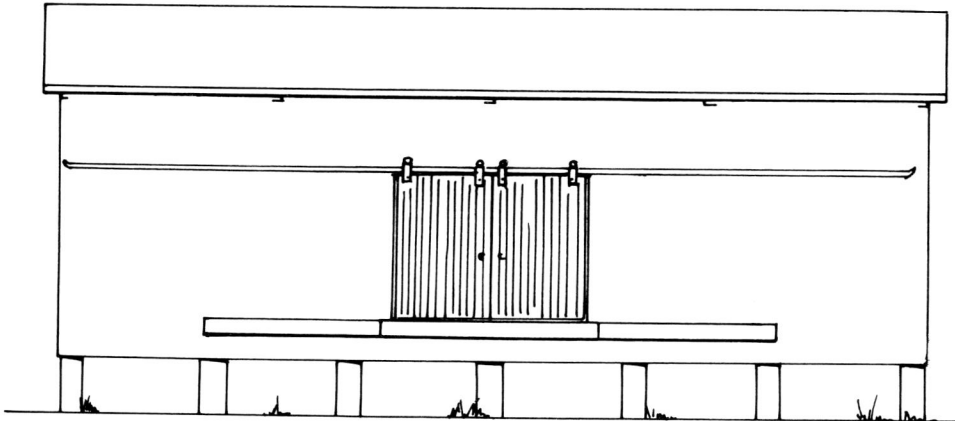

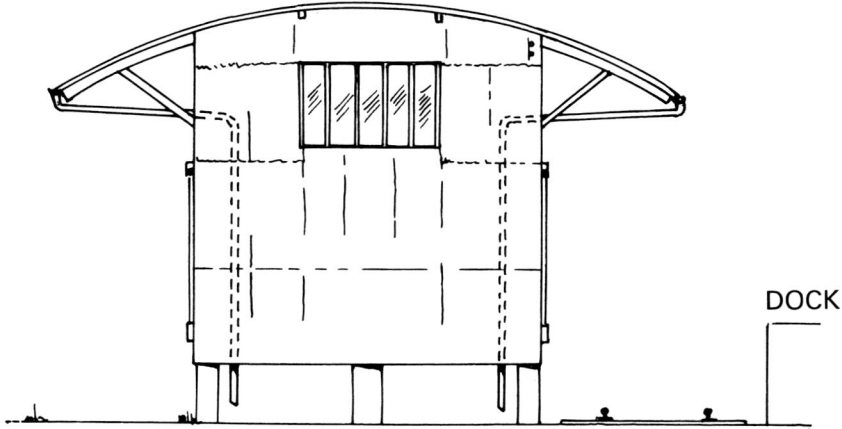

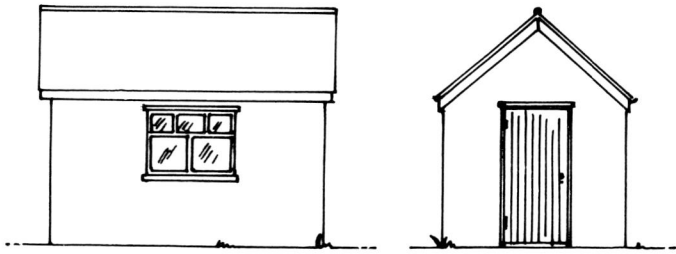

Sketch of Goods shed and Weighbridge Hut at Seahouses.

During the 1939–1945 war, a small signal cabin was built over the ground frame at the Seahouses end of Chathill yard.

Through the years the signals changed from NER wooden post lower quadrant type to standard LNER steel post upper quadrants.

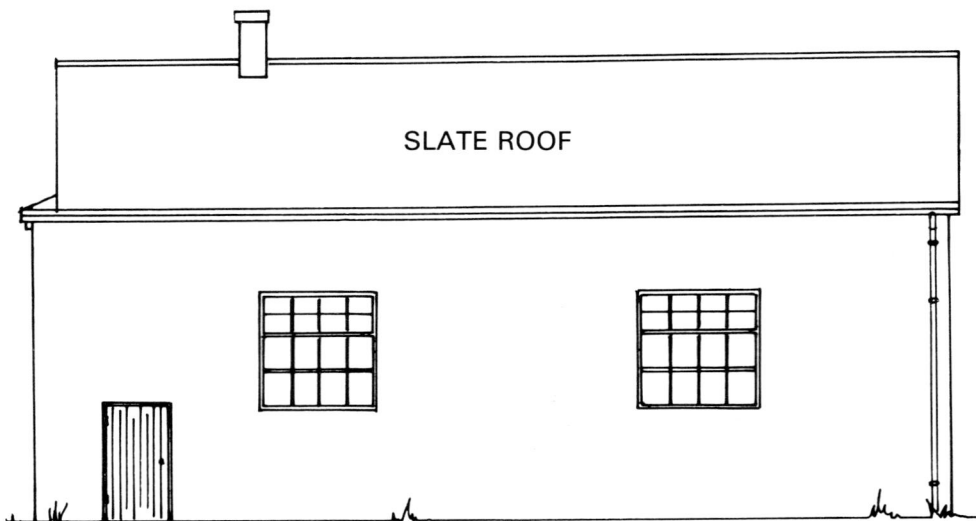

SLATE ROOF

Sketch of Engine shed at Seahouses.

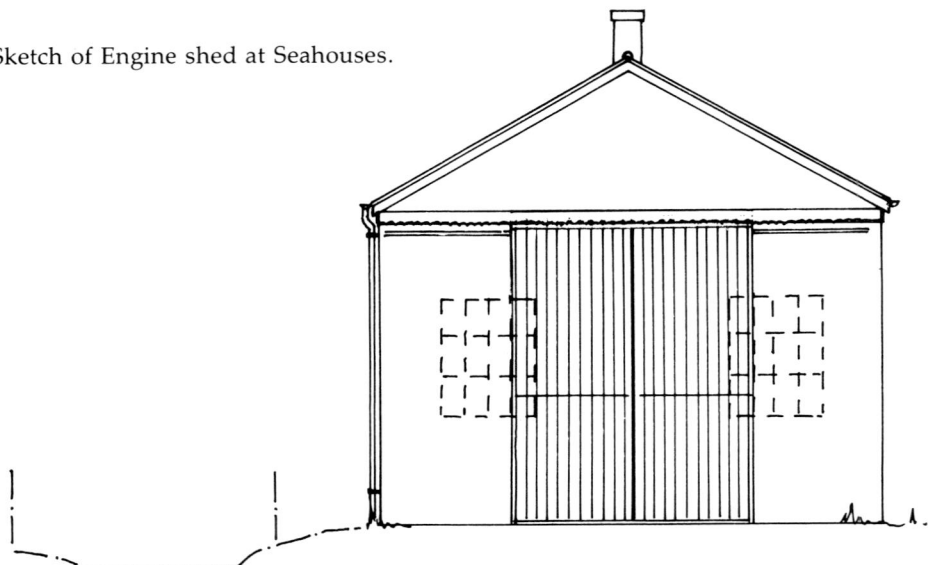

Chapter Five

The Board of Trade Inspection

The first Notice of Inspection was given to the Board of Trade on 27th June, 1898.

On 1st August, 1898 the line was opened for goods traffic and on 10th August the Board of Trade inspected the temporary siding at Chathill.

A certificate regarding the mode of operating the line was sent to the Board of Trade along with the second Notice of Inspection on 7th September. On the 29th the Board of Trade intimated that the inspection would be carried out on 5th October by Colonel Addison. An arrangement was made with the NER for a special train to convey the North Eastern officials, the North Sunderland officials, and others and the NER locomotive was to be used for testing the girders of the underbridge. It is not known which NER locomotive performed this duty. The day of the inspection came and the inspector verbally intimated that alterations were needed to the signals and interlocking at Chathill and that a continuous brake was needed on the coaches. When the official letter came from the Board of Trade the NSR was required to carry out a lot of work before it could start a passenger service. It was pointed out that, as it was hoped excursion traffic would develop, a footbridge should be provided across the main lines at Chathill. Whilst the speed of trains was required to be low to suit the Light Railway Order there were no limitations as to length of trains and, as there were gradients on the line, and in view of the layout at Chathill, the inspector considered it essential that an automatic brake controlled from the locomotive be fitted to the passenger coaches.

The inspection report stated that only one railway had been built but at the commencement at Chathill the line occupied a position intermediate between railways one and two in the deposited plans and was partly outside the limit of deviation number 1. It was also reported that the track consisted of 62 lb. flat bottom rail spiked direct to uncreosoted sleepers. The steepest gradient was given as 1 in 80, the deepest cutting 17 ft and the highest embankment 9 ft. Ash ballast was used which in places was insufficient.

There was one underbridge on the line, a skew span of 18 ft consisting of steel plate girders on cement concrete abutments. Two overbridges, one with a square span of 14 ft and the other a skew span of 18 ft, were of steel trough tops on cement concrete abutments. The two culverts were made in Portland cement concrete and had spans of 9 ft and 6 ft. When the underbridge was tested the girders gave moderate deflections but the inspector remarked that generally the work was satisfactory.

Use was made of the back of the NER down [sic] platform at Chathill, whereas at other places the NSR had built stations which complied with the requirements of the Act. The line was to be worked on the One Engine in Steam principle or by two locomotives coupled together. No signals were provided except at Chathill where the lines to the NER goods yard were crossed. All points on sidings and loops were locked by Annett's key and the NSR had to give a written promise that rolling stock would not be left standing on the passing loop near Chathill – this was necessary because trap points were not provided. The Annett's key was to be incorporated in the train staff.

Action was taken by the NSR and on 11th October a letter was sent to the NER asking Mr Worsdell to "adjust" the brake power on the coaches. The coaches were eventually fitted with the Westinghouse automatic air brake.

On 5th November an undertaking was given to the Board of Trade that vehicles would never stand on the loop and that the NSR were dealing with the roads I and II in the Parish of Bamburgh. (The inspector, whilst agreeing that they were occupation roads rather than public roads, still required them to be dealt with as set out in the Act under level crossings.) They were provided with gates which were kept closed across the roads.

Further information regarding the footbridge at Chathill was sought in a letter to the Board of Trade on 17th November – the bridge was eventually built by the NER.

Having dealt with all the points raised by the Board of Trade inspector, passenger working on the NSR began on 18th December, 1898.

Chapter Six

Locomotives

The first locomotive owned by the NSR was an 0–6–0 saddle tank built by Manning Wardle & Co. Ltd, Boyne Engine Works, Leeds in 1898 and carried their works number 1394. Owing to the financial state of the company the loco was bought on a hire purchase agreement. Costing £1340, the NSR paid £190 to Manning Wardle, the remainder was paid by the Yorkshire Wagon Co. Ltd to whom the NSR made seven annual repayments of £203 13s. 9d.

Carrying the name *Bamburgh* on cast brass plates on each side of the saddle tank, the locomotive was one of the maker's "Class L altered" type and was generally similar to their 1360 built in 1897 for the Selby and Cawood Railway. Basically a standard loco, *Bamburgh* had a large steel cab fitted instead of the more usual weatherboard and was equipped with the Westinghouse air brake. The 3 ft 6 in. diameter wheels were spread over the wheelbase of 10 ft 9 in., the 12 in. by 18 in. cylinders were mounted between the frames with Stephenson link motion to actuate the valves. The frames were directly over the centre of the journals and the leading and intermediate springs were equalised. Pressed to 140 psi, the domeless boiler had a raised top firebox on which the Ramsbottom safety valves were mounted with two escape tubes to lead the steam up through the cab roof. The frames were designed to suit steel bufferbeams instead of the more usual wooden ones and special cast stays were incorporated to suit the Wallaces india-rubber drawbar springs. Screw couplings were fitted, also spring buffers.

The cab was fitted with side screens to protect the crew from the weather and the various fittings were arranged for the driver to stand on the right side. As air brakes were fitted the hand brake was moved to the fireman's side. The air pump was mounted on the right side of the smokebox whilst the reservoir was under the bunker. An injector on the left side of the tank fed the boiler assisted by an axle drive pump on the right side of the locomotive.

Painted green, a light green slightly darker than that used by the North Eastern Railway and lined out with broad black lines edged with white (according to a report in *The Locomotive* of April 1901), the buffers and beams along with the coupling rods were bright red. *Bamburgh* was a pretty little machine and, if not kept in good mechanical order, it was kept clean and polished.

In 1898, before the railway was opened for passenger traffic, *Bamburgh* suffered damage so serious when she was derailed at Chathill that repairs by Manning Wardle were necessary.

To prevent further claims from farmers whose crops had been damaged in a fire caused by sparks a chimney-top spark arrester was

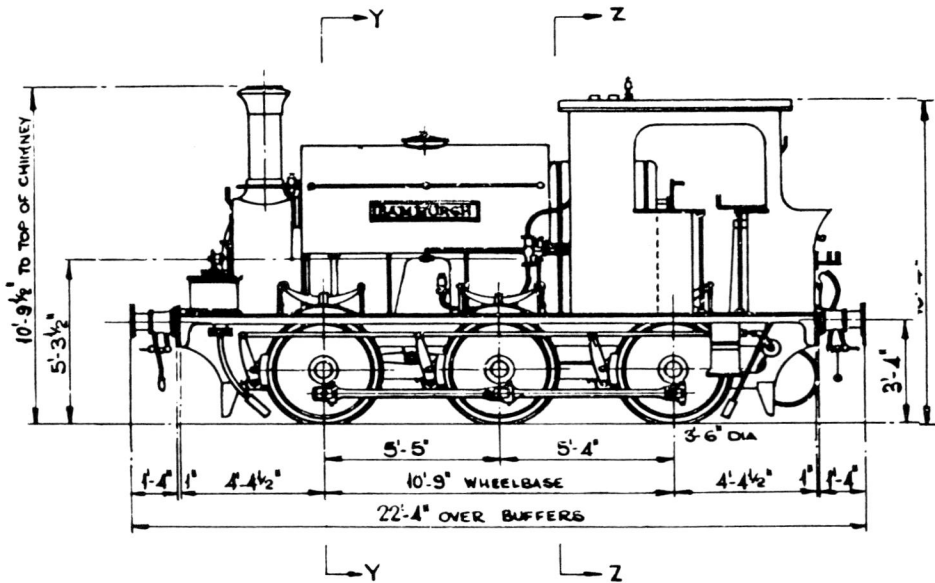

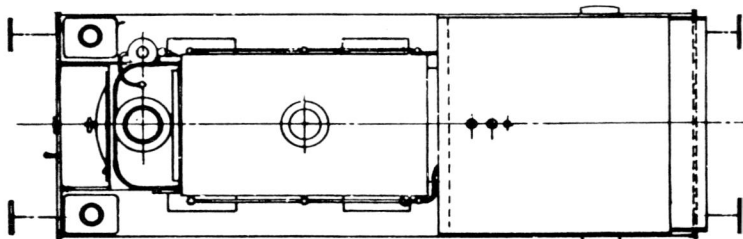

Drawing of locomotive *Bamburgh*.

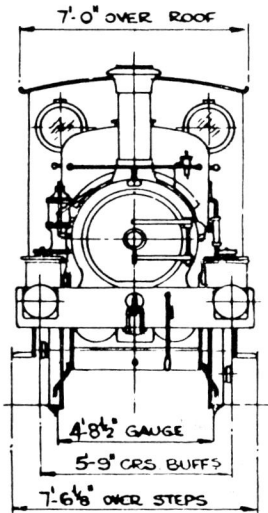

7'-0" OVER ROOF

4'-8½" GAUGE

5'-9" CRS BUFFS

7'-6⅛" OVER STEPS

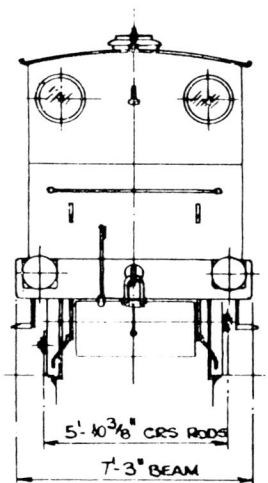

5'-10⅜" CRS RODS

7'-3" BEAM

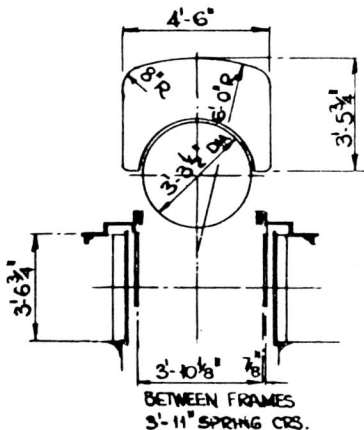

4'-6"

18" R

6'-0" R

3'-5¾"

3'-3¼" DIA

3'-6¾"

3'-10⅛"   ⅞"

BETWEEN FRAMES
3'-11" SPRING CRS.

SECTION AT 'YY'

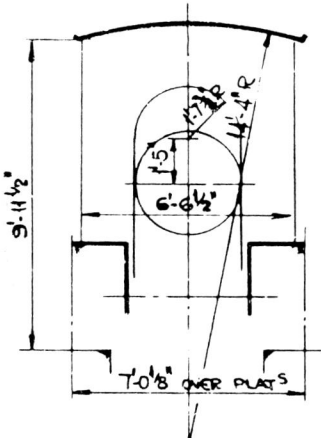

1'-7½" R

4'-4" R

1'-5"

6'-6½"

9'-11½"

7'-0⅛" OVER PLATS

SECTION AT 'ZZ'

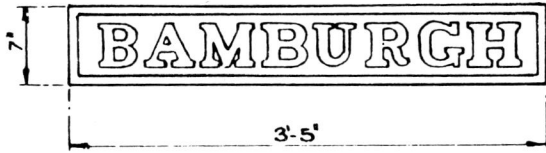

BAMBURGH

7"

3'-5"

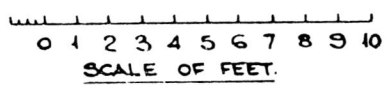

0 1 2 3 4 5 6 7 8 9 10

SCALE OF FEET.

fitted to the locomotive in 1899. *Bamburgh* worked successfully until 16th December, 1902 when, following a failure, she had to go to the NER's Gateshead works whilst an NER locomotive worked the railway. Returned on 29th January, 1903, *Bamburgh* again gave sterling service, but by 1909 the Board were told that a new left cylinder may be needed. No action was taken and in 1913 she was reported to be in so poor a mechanical condition that R & W Hawthorn Leslie sent a representative to examine it with a view to carrying out repairs. March 1914 saw it back in the NER's workshops at Gateshead whilst a locomotive from that Railway hauled the trains between Chathill and Seahouses. Three years later, following the fracture of a crankpin, she again visited Gateshead.

Heavy boiler repairs were necessary in 1920 and *Bamburgh* this time journeyed back to its maker's works at Leeds where a new steel boiler and smokebox tubeplate were fitted to the old smokebox. A new inner firebox made from copper was also fitted along with new brass tubes. The original feed pump must not have been too successful in service as the Manning Wardle repair book states that a new injector and gear was fitted to replace one "not our make", the steam connections being on the left side of the locomotive. Costing £2953 10*s*. 0*d*. with carriage at £50 16*s*. 7*d*. the repair of the locomotive was set out against the Government as payment for the period under their control. Whilst away from its native heath, *Bamburgh* was replaced by a locomotive again hired from the NER.

Back in service *Bamburgh* must have been kept running until she wouldn't run any more, and, following a report that the locomotive was unsafe she was sent to Gateshead whilst No. 407 from the NER relieved her on 11th August, 1926. In the works it was found that the tubeplate was very badly wasted, wasted beyond the limit at which it could be built up by welding and the condition of the wheel sets was questionable. Other repairs included repairs to brake gear, air pump and boiler mountings. On 10th October, 1926 NER No. 407 worked the 4.10 pm train from Seahouses to Chathill, where it was exchanged for *Bamburgh* which then pulled the 5.42 pm train to Seahouses.

In 1933 boiler repairs were again necessary along with attention to the brasses and springs. After receiving quotations from Armstrong Whitworth's and Hawthorn Leslie's the work was given to an engineer at North Sunderland called Hughes who had a small workshop in the village. The boiler was removed and sent to Kitsons on 15th November, 1933. These repairs were called for by the NER loco inspectors who banned *Bamburgh* from their tracks until she was put into proper order. Meanwhile a 'J79' was hired at £10 per week, this time No. 1787 was sent to the line. Whilst this locomotive was on loan

Meyer learned that Armstrong Whitworth's were willing to loan a four wheeled diesel electric locomotive for £8 per week so this offer was accepted. After the decision to purchase a diesel locomotive in 1934 consideration was given to the sale of *Bamburgh*. However, better sense prevailed and she was kept as a spare locomotive for use when the diesel was out of use for repairs or maintenance.

Once the line was under LNER control the new management gave *Bamburgh* an overhaul at Darlington and she returned to the railway again to act as a spare locomotive. During World War II, with the amount of traffic handled increasing, the necessity for two locomotives in use at the same time arose, and once more *Bamburgh* saw regular daily use. As she had to haul heavier loads than ever before wear and tear soon took their toll. In 1944 she visited Tweedmouth sheds for minor repairs and in the following year another visit to Darlington occurred. 1946 saw her on Tweedside for the second time, whilst in July 1947, following a fractured crankpin, she again journeyed to Gateshead. Back in service at Seahouses she was steamed for what was to be the last time on 25th September when she burst a cylinder. The 'Y7' then on hire from the LNER had to work all trains as the NSR diesel was already at Darlington. Estimates for repairs to the steamer were obtained but proved to be too high so she was pushed into the end of the long siding at Seahouses – a forlorn sight to those who knew her in her heyday. Rusting away she remained there until 11th October, 1949, when she left for scrapping at Glasgow by the Motherwell Machinery and Scrap Co. who had bought her for £71 against a weight of 20 tons. Carriage was to be paid by the NSR and, dogged as usual by misfortune, that bill came to £52 10s. 1d. On her way to the scrapyard she ran hot at Edinburgh and required attention to her axleboxes! The NSR's proceeds from the sale – £18 9s. 11d.

In the early 1930s the Newcastle firm of Armstrong Whitworth & Co. Ltd were pioneering diesel electric traction and built a small shunting locomotive to demonstrate their patented ABE transmission. The locomotive had been on loan to a steelworks at Scunthorpe and on show at the 1933 Shipping and Machinery Exhibition in London where she ran up and down a 100 yd length of track using British produced gas oil as fuel. In November 1933 she arrived at Chathill having had windscreens fitted to give the driver some protection. Told that the locomotive could not be fitted with air brakes for the train the NSR were not worried – they had operated unbraked passenger trains fairly regularly since 1914 – so into use she went.

Weighing 15 tons and rated at 75 horse power, the locomotive had the engine and generator mounted across the frames at the front end, the traction motor mounted behind it drove onto a jackshaft which

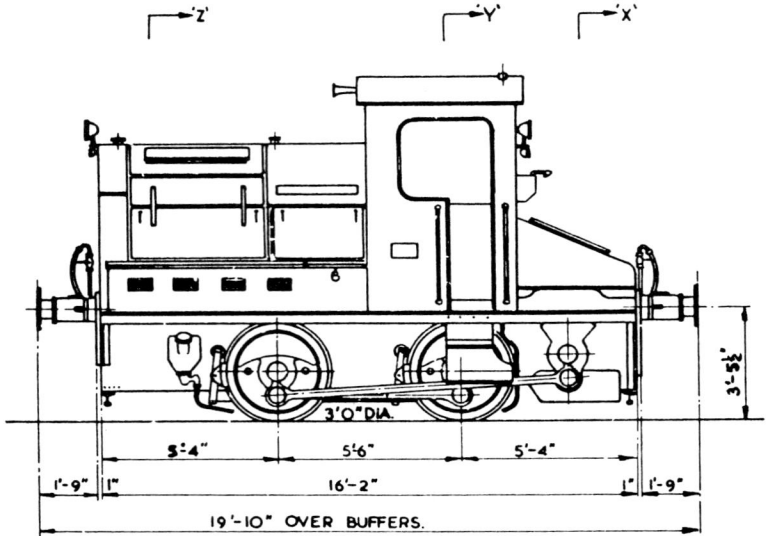

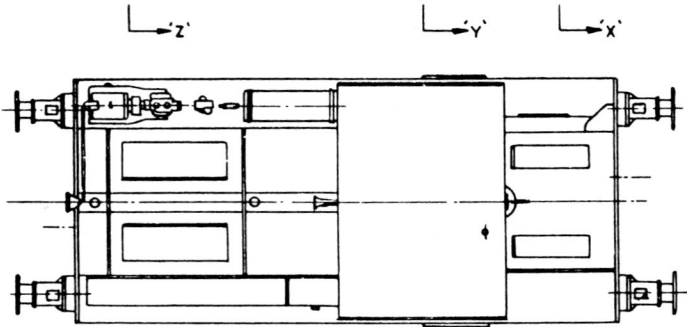

Drawing of locomotive *The Lady Armstrong*.

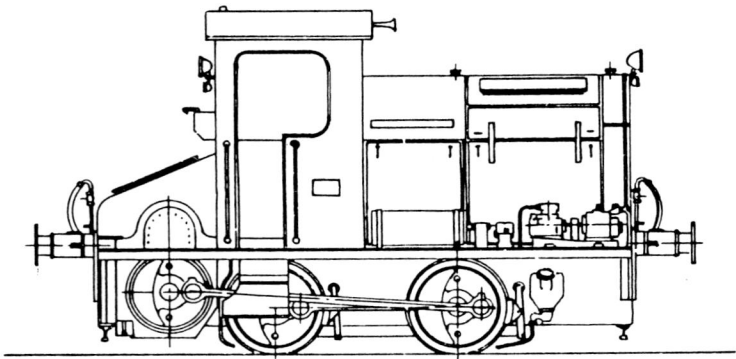

Bamburgh at North Sunderland after overhaul, June 1934.

H.C. Casserley

Bamburgh at Seahouses, August 1921, after overhaul at Leeds. The weigh-bridge cabin can be seen behind the warehouse.   *Author's Collection*

Bamburgh at Seahouses on 8th October, 1900. Note the high level air pipe connection.   *Ken Nunn*

Bamburgh at North Sunderland in June 1934 after recent overhaul. Note the grounded body of NER "birdcage" behind the locomotive.   *H.C. Casserley*

Bamburgh seen here dumped at Seahouses after withdrawal. Note the wood block wedged in to hold up the nameplate in position.   *Author's Collection*

The nameplate, ex 0–6–0ST on the GER coach.   *Author*

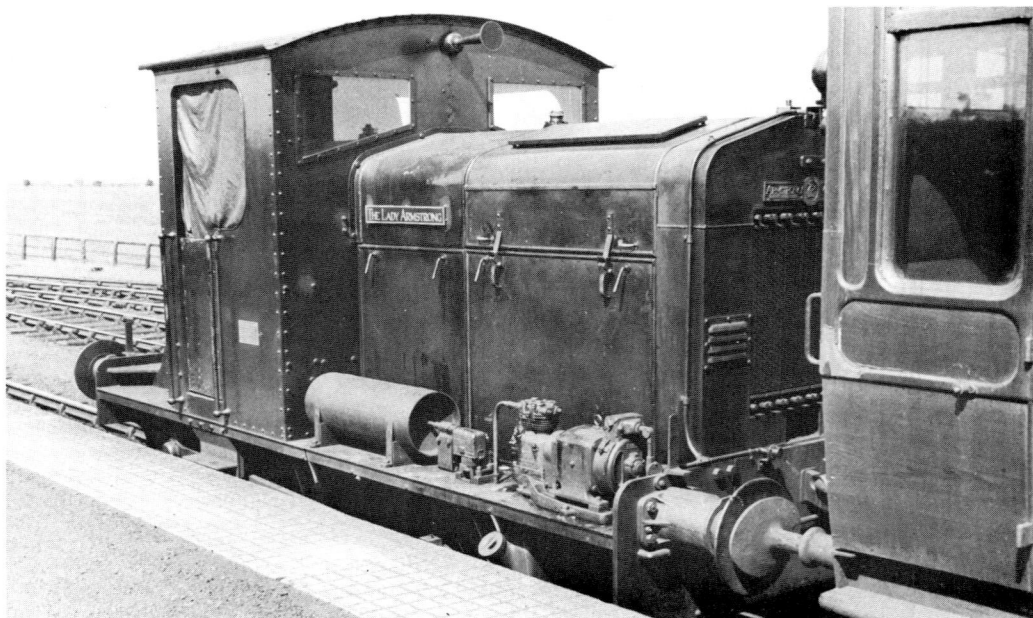

A fine view of *The Lady Armstrong*, showing the air reservoir for the train brakes and the jumper socket for coach lights.   *H.N. James*

The right hand side of the sister engine. This engine is now preserved in full working order on the Tanfield Railway.   *Author*

The left hand side of *The Lady Armstrong* photographed here at Seahouses in June 1934. *H.C. Casserley*

The Armstrong Whitworth nameplate, as carried above the radiator. *Author*

The Lady Armstrong on a passenger train alongside the LNER No. 986 in the
loop at Seahouses. *Author's Collection*

The demonstrator diesel locomotive at Chathill Station with the ex-NER
birdcage brake coach and wagons. *Author's Collection*

The ex-BR Class 'Y7' No. 68089 as *Eve* on the Harbour and General Works at Morecambe in March 1955. *Author's Collection*

LNER Class 'J79' No. 1787 seen here on the Bowes Railway as No. 5 at Wardley Colliery. *L.G. Charlton*

A side view of BR Class 'Y7' No. 68089 outside Seahouses Shed.
Author's Collection

LMS Class 'OF' No. 11217 a similar locomotive as used on the North Sunderland in 1948.
Author's Collection

4'-8½" GAUGE.

5'-8¼"

8'-0" MAX. WIDTH.

10'-0"

7'-4"

6"R

4'-2"

4'-1½"

4'-6"

5'-4"

3'-3"

7'-8"

SECTION 'ZZ'

7'-10" RAD.

4"

6'-10"

10'-1"

4'-5⅜"

5½"

8'-0"

SECTION 'YY'

4'-4¼"

SECTION 'XX'

0 1 2 3 4 5 6 7

SCALE OF FEET.

ARMSTRONG WHITWORTH

RADIATOR NAMEPLATE.

5'-6"

6"

3'-3"

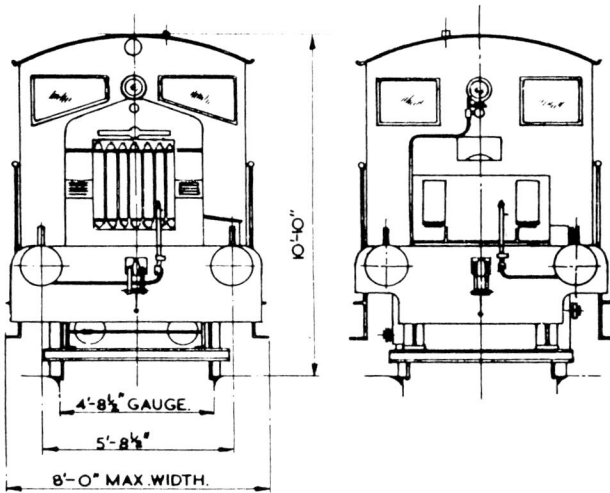

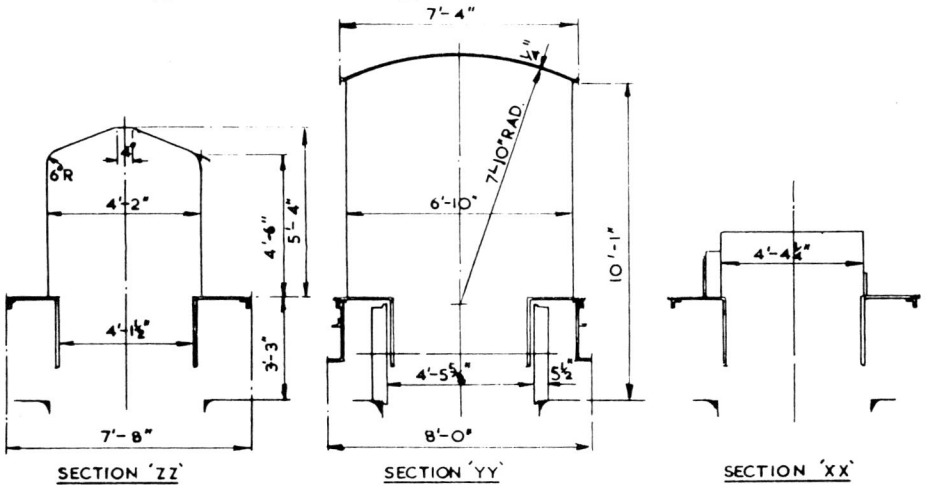

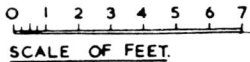

AXLE & JACKSHAFT CENTRES.

transmitted the drive via a scotch yoke to the rail wheels. Straight air brake equipment was fitted and the locomotive could be driven from the footboard alongside the wheels or from the cab. The ABE transmission claimed simplicity of design and maintenance, the makers stated that any mechanic used to working on lorries could deal efficiently with the locomotive. The Armstrong Saurer engine was capable of running at speeds between an idle of approximately 450 rpm and a maximum governed speed of 2000 rpm. The generator was compound wound and was coupled through a reverser to the traction motor. The driver's throttle lever was connected to the fuel pump on the engine and all control of speed etc. was made by that lever in the same manner as locomotives which nowadays use a three stage torque convertor as a transmission. There was no field weakening or resistance control of the electric transmission.

Some interesting facts on the locomotive's performance on the NSR were published in the Diesel Traction Supplement of the *Railway Gazette* in August 1934 where it was stated that by using diesel traction the company hoped to save some £300 per year. On loan for some six months, the locomotive covered close on 6000 miles hauling trains of one or two coaches and in some cases wagons as well. The heaviest load hauled was 90 tons, but in shunting operations 200 tons were moved. A weekly mileage of 280 used 60 gallons of fuel and 4½ gallons of lubricating oil. Preparation and maintenance time per week was between six and eight hours and during its service on the railway the locomotive required one new set of brake blocks, two pistons and one cylinder head.

In 1933 Armstrong Whitworths built five somewhat similar locomotives using the same engine and transmission and one was offered to the NSR on hire purchase terms. Costing £1850, the railway paid £1000 in cash and the rest was paid off by February 1936. Named *"The Lady Armstrong"*, the NSR loco was numbered D25 by the makers and was delivered by them in mid-1934. The engine and generator were mounted along the line of the locomotive and the cab was situated towards the centre of the locomotive in the manner now considered up to date for shunting locomotives. The traction motor was mounted across the frames behind the cab with the driving pinion on the right side. The jackshaft pinion was made from a wheel centre of the same type as the road wheels but instead of a tyre it was fitted with a spur gear. On the left side a conventional flycrank was fitted. The drive was taken to the leading wheels thence to the trailers by coupling rods fitted with self aligning roller bearings. The control desk was mounted across the front wall of the cab and the batteries were in a box on the left platform. The right platform was occupied by a small electrically driven compressor, its governor, and the auxiliary air reservoir. A headlight and a ruby marker were fitted at each end of the locomotive and air brake equipment was installed for controlling the train. Provision was made on each buffer beam for coupling up a jumper cable from the coaches so feeding the electric lights fitted to them. Painted black with red buffers and beams and with polished rods, the locomotive was of very smart appearance. The Saurer engine was rated at 85 bhp at 2000 rpm, and the Laurence Scott and Electromotors generator and traction motor were modified from standard to give the locomotive a maximum speed of 30 mph.

Everyone was pleased with the locomotive when delivered but by 1938 crankshaft breakages were occurring and on one occasion the locomotive was returned to the makers for repair. In 1940 she journeyed to Darlington for repairs including a new crankshaft and pistons. When returned the staff seemed to think that she was in poorer mechanical condition than before she left and battery trouble became more common resulting in the locomotive failing often and requiring hauling back to Seahouses for battery charging. The locomotive was out of use from 1st January to 12th April on that occasion. When she arrived on the NSR the locomotive bonnet faced east. Not being acceptable that way round she was run down the main line one day to Alnmouth to be turned on the turntable. After being twice under repair at Seahouses she went back to Darlington on 6th September following derailment damage; not until the end of January 1941 did she run over her own track again.

Throughout the war she was available for traffic on the average of one week in two but when working she gave yeoman service. In 1946 severe damage occurred to the Saurer engine and in the October she went to Darlington works from which she never emerged again. New or second-hand parts for the locomotive were not readily available, and, as repairs would be too expensive, she was eventually sold to Arnott Young and Co. for scrap in October 1949, bringing the NSR the grand sum of £42 10s. 0d. Before deciding to let her go the NSR management did look around for a suitable second-hand locomotive but none were to be had. Of the other four locos of the type, one was scrapped in 1964, one in 1966, whilst the other two are still in existence. One of these is presently in the National Railway Museum at York whilst the other, although having had the Saurer engine replaced by a Gardner, is preserved in full working order on the Tanfield Railway. One cannot help thinking that if *The Lady Armstrong* had gone to a locomotive builder who was used to the whims of diesel traction in 1946 she could well have been in service at the closure of the line, in fact that fateful day may have been put off for a year or two.

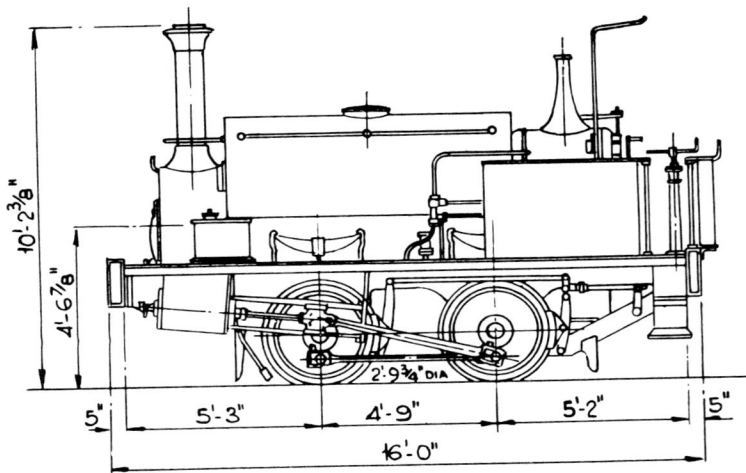

10'-2³/₈"
4'-6⁷/₈"

2'-9¾" DIA

5" 5'-3" 4'-9" 5'-2" 5"
16'-0"

MANNING WARDLE LOCO 1074 OF 1888.

NO DETAILS OF BUFFERS AND DRAWGEAR ARE AVAILABLE.

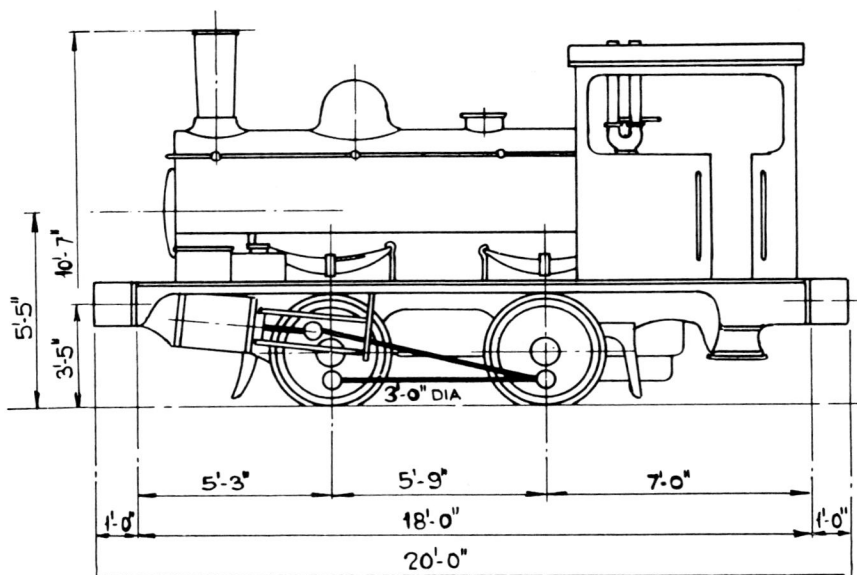

10'-7"
5'-5"
3'-5"

3'-0" DIA

5'-3" 5'-9" 7'-0"
1'-0" 18'-0" 1'-0"
20'-0"

LMSR CLASS "OF" LOCOMOTIVE (Ex L&YR).

CYLINDERS	13" DIA x 18" STROKE	HEATING SURFACE	475.75 SQ.FT.
BOILER PRESSᴱ	160 LB/SQ IN	GRATE AREA	
TRACTIVE EFFORT	11,335 LB.	WEIGHT – STEAM UP	21T 5C

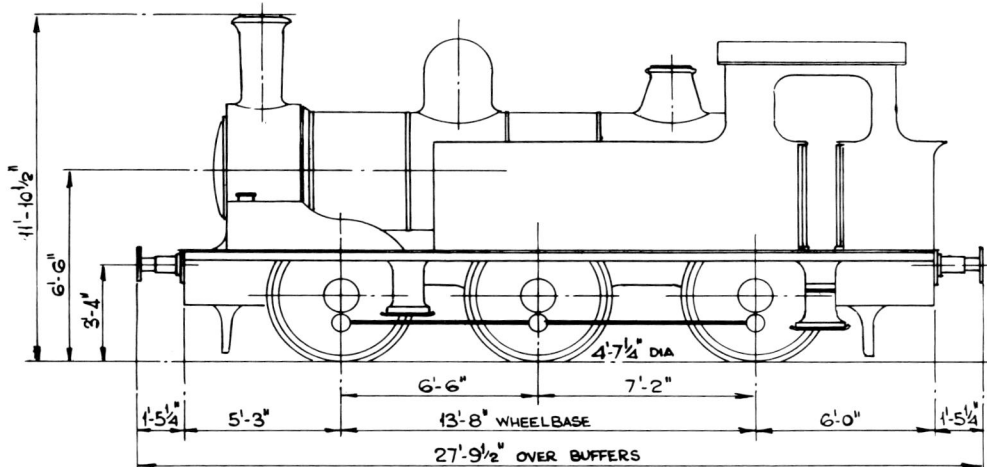

LNER CLASS J71 LOCOMOTIVE.

CYLINDERS	16" DIA x 22" STROKE	HEATING SURFACE	731 SQ. FT.
BOILER PRESS^E	140 LB/SQ IN.	GRATE AREA	11.3 SQ. FT
TRACTIVE EFFORT	12,130 LB	WEIGHT – STEAM UP	36T 13C 2Q

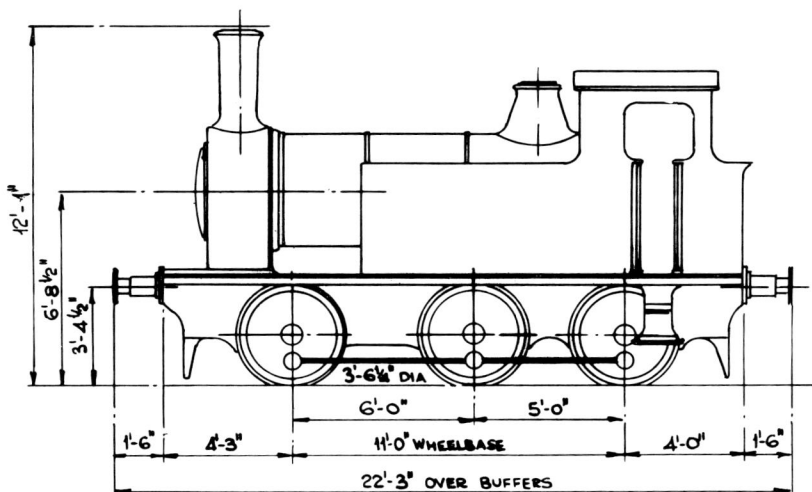

LNER CLASS J79 LOCOMOTIVE.

CYLINDERS	14" DIA x 20" STROKE	HEATING SURFACE	505 SQ. FT
BOILER PRESS^E	140 LB/SQ IN.	GRATE AREA	11.3 SQ. FT
TRACTIVE EFFORT	11,040 LB.	WEIGHT– STEAM UP	25T. OC

When the NSR's own motive power was out of use locomotives were hired from the NER and LNER. Until their sale in the late 1930s the small 0–6–0 tank locos of class 'H2' or LNER 'J79' were first choice. With typical NER appearance these inside cylinder locos were in effect a six-wheeled version of the earlier NER class 'H'. The wheels, cylinders and domeless boiler were standard with that class but the Joy's motion and connecting rods were three inches longer on the six-wheelers than on the four-coupled design. The locomotives loaned to the NSR, Nos. 407 and 1787, were fitted with automatic air brakes for the train, but with only a handbrake in the locomotive. No. 407 had larger side tanks fitted when loaned to the Selby and Cawood Railway, both locomotives had the air brake pump fitted in the cab.

During World War II, when the need for a second locomotive arose at a time when only one NSR machine was available, experiments were carried out with an LNER single speed Sentinel shunting locomotive. On trip workings the locomotive proved to be slow and could not keep the timings, on some occasions it was necessary to stop and "blow up" steam. A similar two-speed locomotive of LNER class 'Y3', fitted with a vacuum brake, also proved unsatisfactory and the experiment was discontinued.

The next locomotive sent to the railway for a trial was as a result of the NSR management asking the LNER if they had a suitable small six-wheeled locomotive fitted with the Westinghouse brake available for hire. In reply the LNER said the smallest locomotive they could supply with a continuous brake, the vacuum brake, was a 'J71', a former NER six-coupled side tank. In 1944, No. 1690 arrived at Chathill for service on the railway but, after two derailments due to the long wheelbase spreading the track on the curve at Chathill, the locomotive was returned to Newcastle.

An 0–4–0 locomotive was then tried out on the railway, a class 'Y7' side tank. In fact this was the NER class 'H', the six-coupled versions of which had given such good service in the past. After proving that this type of locomotive could handle both passenger and freight trains, the NSR paid the LNER £90 to have a vacuum ejector and piping, also a windscreen on the open cab back, fitted to LNER No. 986 so that she could be hired. A locomotive of this class was on hire throughout 1946 and at one period both Nos. 982 and 986 were in use on the railway; not being brake fitted, No. 982 was not allowed to work passenger trains.

Renumbered 8089, former 986 worked on the railway throughout 1947 and in the autumn of 1948, when repairs were necessary, she was replaced by an L & Y "Pug", LMS No. 11217. Unfitted and indeed dumb-buffered, this loco was used on goods and fish trains only. During the time the 'Y7' was out of use Beecroft's taxis provided the passenger services. Returned to service, No. 8089, later renumbered

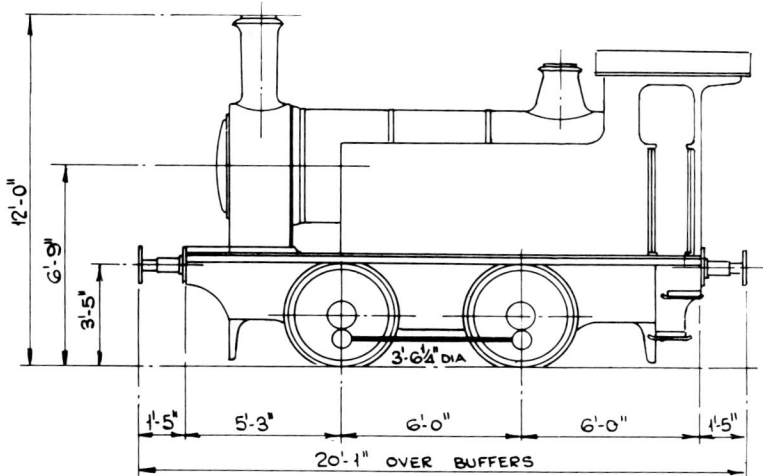

LNER CLASS Y7 LOCOMOTIVE.

12'-0"
6'-9"
3'-5"
3'-6¼" DIA
1'-5" 5'-3" 6'-0" 6'-0" 1'-5"
20'-1" OVER BUFFERS

CYLINDERS	14" DIA x 22" STROKE	HEATING SURFACE	505 SQ. FT.
BOILER PRESSᴱ	140 LB/SQ IN.	GRATE AREA	11·3 SQ. FT.
TRACTIVE EFFORT	11,040 LB.	WEIGHT – STEAM UP	21T 13C 3Q.

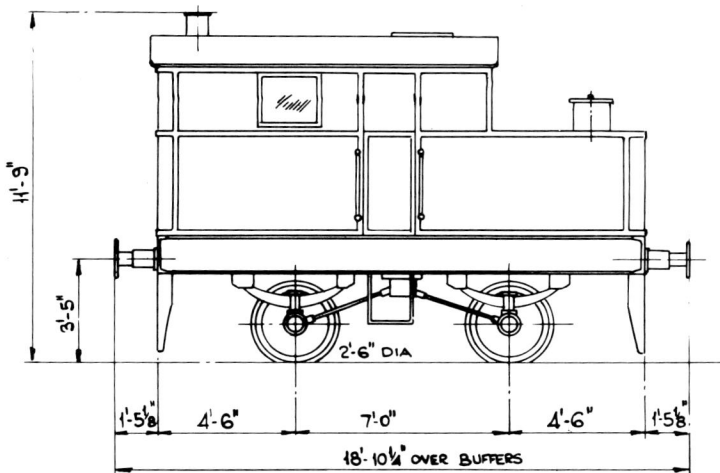

LNER CLASS Y1 & Y3 LOCOMOTIVE

11'-9"
3'-5"
2'-6" DIA
1'-5⅝" 4'-6" 7'-0" 4'-6" 1'-5⅝"
18'-10¼" OVER BUFFERS

CYLINDERS		6¾" DIA x 9" STROKE	HEATING SURFACE		71·5 SQ. FT.
BOILER PRESSURE		275 LB/SQ IN.	GRATE AREA		5·1 SQ FT.
TRACTIVE EFFORT	-Y1	7,260 LB	WEIGHT – STEAM UP	Y1	19T 16C
	Y3	12,600 LB & 4705 LB.		Y3	20T 16C

68089 by British Railways, worked the trains with only occasional spells out of use for repair until the line closed in 1951 when she returned to British Railways by whom she was sold to Harbour and General Works. Fitted with a bunker and named *Eve,* she was sent to Morecambe to work on a sea wall contract on the completion of which she was cut up. Those who knew the locomotive on the NSR and remarked on her immaculate condition (the Railway Executive Motive Power Officer once complimented the crew on the manner in which they looked after her) must have felt very sorry indeed to see her in her last few days.

It is rather surprising that in their search for motive power the BR management only once went outside of the North Eastern Region. There were quite a few suitable locomotives in use on the LNER at the time, for instance the small 0–4–2 tanks used at the Aberdeen docks seemed suitable candidates. It is interesting to record that in August 1946 the LNER offered to rebuild No. 986 as an 0–6–0 tank and sell it to the NSR for £1370, but as the management were aware that it was an obsolete locomotive and spares were not available, they turned the offer down.

Two other locomotives remain to be described, both of which worked over the NSR but were owned by the contractors variously building and demolishing the railway.

Whilst it cannot be confirmed, it is most probable that Whitaker Bros used a small Manning Wardle four-coupled saddle tank whilst building the railway. This locomotive was built in 1888, carried the works number 1074, and was of the builder's "Class F altered" type. The four wheels were 2 ft 9¾ in. in diameter at 4 ft 9 in. centres. The cylinders, outside the frames, were 10 in. diameter by 16 in. stroke and, like *Bamburgh,* the valves were actuated by Stephenson's valve gear. The boiler was domeless with Salter safety valves mounted on top of the raised firebox. Pressed to 120 pounds per square inch, the boiler was fed by an injector and eccentric driven feed pump. A hand brake only was fitted with cast iron blocks acting on all wheels. No cab was provided, the driver having to shelter behind a weatherboard. Dumb buffers were fitted at each end of the locomotive and the coupling chains were provided with hooks on the third link.

The last locomotive to run over the railway was a Ruston and Hornsby four-wheel chain-coupled diesel mechanical locomotive owned by the Motherwell Machinery and Scrap Co. Ltd. This locomotive hauled British Railways wagons into which the steel scrap recovered was loaded, and upon completion of the demolition returned to its owner's Motherwell yard. This locomotive had a 48 horse power diesel engine and was to the maker's standard design, class 48 DS. Unfortunately it has not been possible to positively identify this locomotive.

Chapter Seven
Rolling Stock

Mr Scott, one of the Directors, accompanied the Company's Secretary to Inverness in June 1898 to inspect five four-wheeled coaches which the Highland Railway were offering for sale. These were priced at £70 each and, before committing themselves, the Directors, conscious of the need to conserve their assets, wanted to know if the price included the cleaning, varnishing, the general overhaul of each vehicle, and the conversion of No. 110 to a brake composite. The other coaches were numbered 103, 106, 108 and 109. After discussion the Board decided to purchase these vehicles and on September 20th they were delivered to Chathill, still in Highland livery but bearing the initials N.S.R.

Although precise details of these coaches are not known, details have been culled from the only two known photographs showing three of them in use on NSR in 1900. The numbers referred to, 103, 106, 108, 109 and 110, apply to Highland Railway class 'G' rib-sided coaches. It is thought, however, that the numbers were sale numbers and were not those carried in service. Sketches have been prepared showing details of the three known vehicles, it should be noted that these sketches are not to scale and accuracy cannot be guaranteed. They do, however, give an idea of appearances (*page 61*).

Following the Board of Trade inspection the vacuum brake with which the coaches were fitted was replaced by Westinghouse automatic air brake equipment (by the NER) and, when completed, passenger traffic was commenced on 12th December. Four days later the coaches were sold by the NSR to the Yorkshire Wagon and Finance Company for £150 each so providing the Board with a little bit more cash to help meet the contractor's bill. It was not until February 1906 that the repayments were complete. Meanwhile three of the coaches were repainted in the middle of 1900 and two old sails were purchased late in 1901 to protect the two spare coaches from the ravages of the elements.

The next items of rolling stock (if they could be included in that category) were a platelayers' trolley and velocipede purchased for a total of £10 at the plant sale from Lord Londonderry's railway in 1901. Used by the platelayers, these two items were still in stock fifty years later when the railway closed.

Only a few months, after the Highland coaches had been purchased for the second time, complaints were received over their condition. Once again Mr Scott and the Secretary went inspecting second-hand coaching stock, this time to see some old Mersey Railway vehicles made redundant following that railway's electrification, and two North Eastern vehicles at York. The Mersey vehicles were

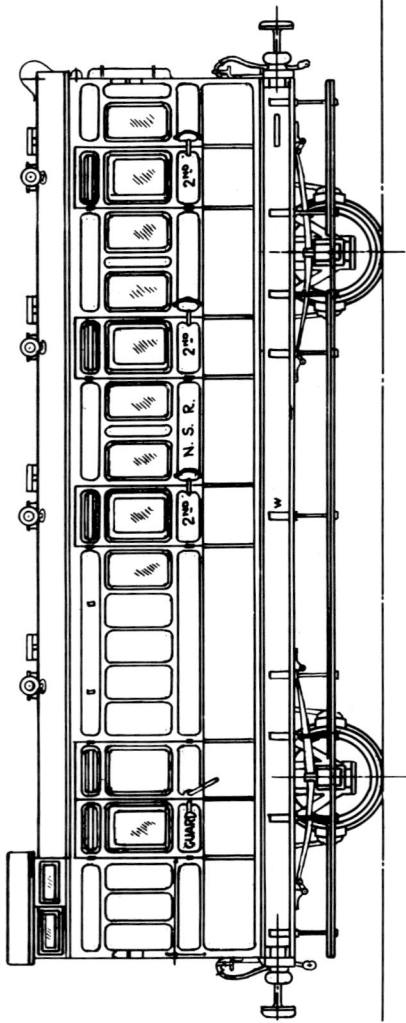

30' 0" BRAKE SECOND CARRIAGE AS RUNNING IN 1933

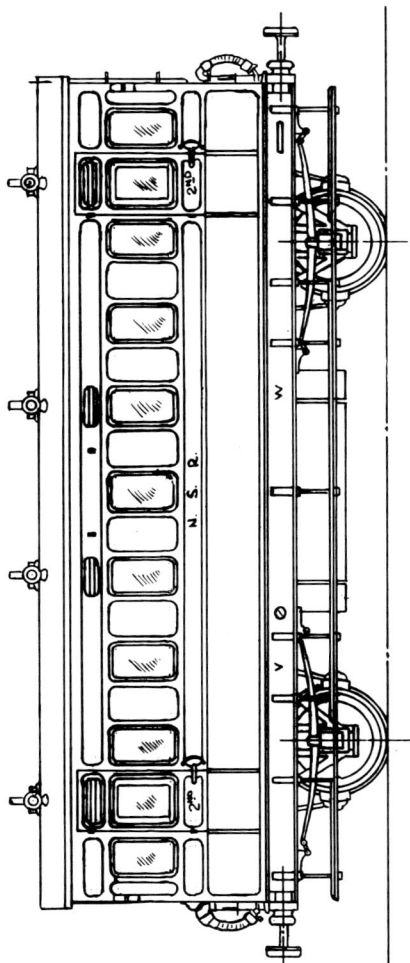

28' 0" SALOON SECOND CARRIAGE

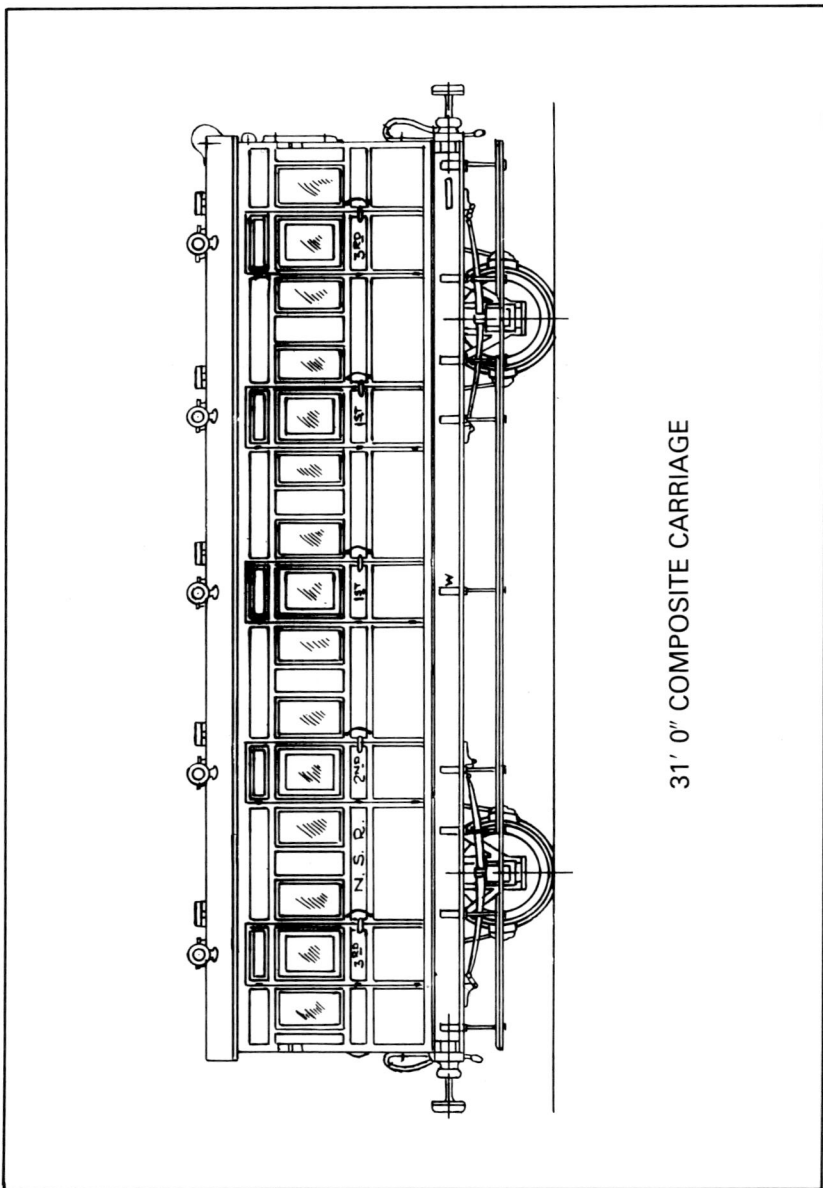

31' 0" COMPOSITE CARRIAGE

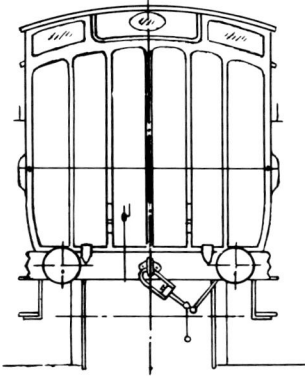

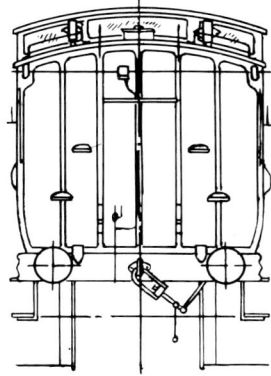

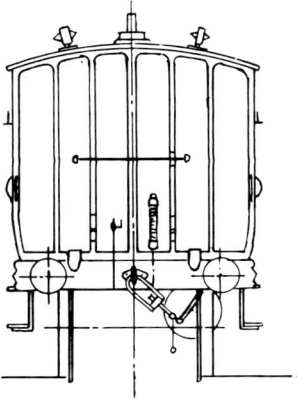

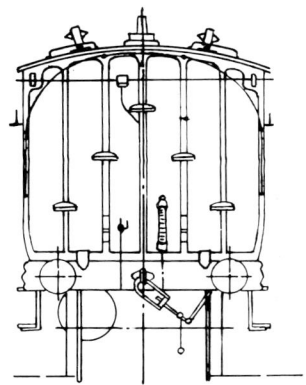

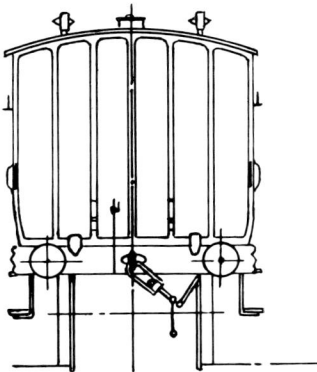

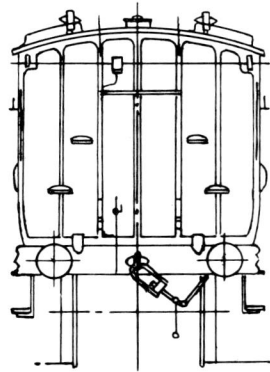

Scale of Feet

0 1 2 3 4 5 6 7 8 9 10

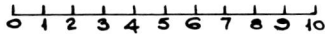

End views of the carriages shown on previous pages.

not considered suitable for use on the NSR, whilst the NER stock was rejected on account of cost. The main line company agreed to repair and paint two of the Highland's at a cost of £20 to £25 each; three coaches actually visited Walkergate shops and in due course the NSR received a bill for £164 17s. 4d. About 1911 two of the coaches were converted to open wagons for stone traffic from the Pasture Hill Quarry, the remainder being sold for a total of £38 10s. 2d. in 1913.

In 1911 a coach was bought second-hand from the NER. Offered to them at £70 the Board wished to know if this price included thorough overhauling, painting inside and out, lettering, roof recovered, wheels turned, bearings attended to and delivery to Chathill. A satis-factory answer must have been received because the coach duly arrived on the NSR. Built by the NER in 1883 and numbered 1980, the coach complied with diagram 58. The body was 30 ft long and 7 ft 11 in. wide. The wheelbase was 19 ft. Seating capacity was 50 in five compartments, air brakes were fitted and the compartments were oil lit. Painted mid-brown and lettered in yellow it was branded as a first, second and third class composite by its new owners. This vehicle remained in service until 1937 and in 1938 the body was sold and the underframe scrapped.

The next vehicle to appear on the railway was a North Eastern Railway four-wheeled brake third with a raised lantern or "birdcage" over the outer end of the brake compartment. Purchased in 1912 for £76, it had been built by the NER and conformed to diagram X. The seating capacity was thirty in three compartments. It was built in 1884 and was 30 ft long over the body with a width over body of 7 ft 11 in. Like the compartment coach it was fitted with the air brake and was oil lit. It was painted by the NSR in a similar livery to the coach and was branded second class. In 1934 the vehicle was withdrawn, the body being made into a bothie at North Sunderland and the under-frame was scrapped. The handbrake wheel and rigging was trans-ferred to the saloon which was converted to a brake composite at that time (see later).

By 1921 the two coaches were in need of tyre turning and other sundry repairs. Two similar types of vehicle were hired from the North Eastern allowing the NSR vehicles to be lifted and the wheel sets removed for shipment to the Leeds Wheel and Axle Company who fitted new tyres to all wheel sets and new axles to two wheel sets.

A further North Eastern coach was purchased from Watts, Hardy and Company, Howdon-on-Tyne, in 1924 for £90. Before the coming of the motor bus and char-a-banc office outings were catered for in saloon coaches. Seats were arranged all round the sides of the coach and folding tables were arranged down the middle. Third class

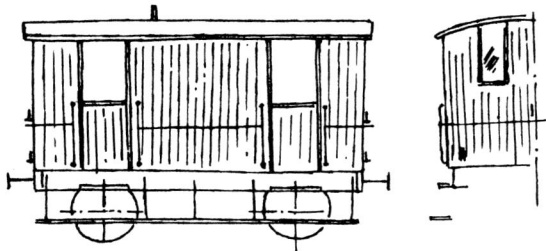

NORTH BRITISH RAILWAY 10T BRAKE VAN.

NOTE
THIS COACH IS
HIGHER THAN THE
OTHER TWO SHOWN
IN PHOTOGRAPHS.

DOORS HUNG
ON LEFT.

EX HIGHLAND COACH 'NO 110' AS CONVERTED TO A BRAKE THIRD.

DOORS HUNG
ON LEFT.

EX HIGHLAND COACH, THOUGHT TO HAVE BEEN A FAMILY SALOON.

COPIES OF SKETCHES OF VEHICLES
WHICH CANNOT BE IDENTIFIED

DOORS HUNG
ON LEFT

EX HIGHLAND COACH, THOUGHT TO HAVE BEEN A FIRST CLASS COACH.

Sketches of Highland coaches and North British van.

saloons did not have lavatory accommodation. The new acquisition was a vehicle of this type. Fitted with both air and vacuum brakes and gas lit the coach was built by the NER in 1888 to diagram 61. Unlike the other ex-North Eastern coaches this one was carried on spoked wheels, however the wooden faced buffers were common to all three. The NSR painted it in their now standard brown livery and upgraded the coach from third class to second class. This vehicle gained notoriety in the popular press in the early thirties, when comment was made on the cretonne curtains at the windows and the carpet on the floor.

When in 1933 Mr Meyer was appointed General Manager of the railway, he proposed to the Board that a new coach be bought and the saloon be converted to a brake second. No new rolling stock was acquired at that time, but in 1934, when the birdcage was withdrawn, the handbrake fittings were taken out and put into the saloon. At the newly formed brake end the sides were removed between the doors and the ends and new doors made from tongued and grooved wood were fitted. On one side the existing door was moved towards the end to avoid re-hanging it. This was very similar to the manner in which the Highland Railway altered the third class coach No. 110. A partition was put across the van at the end of the seats and electric lighting, fed from the diesel locomotive by a light jumper cable, was fitted in both compartments. In this form the coach remained in service and was used as a brake van for both passenger and goods trains until the railway passed into LNER control. Inspection by the latter revealed that this vehicle did not have a brake cock in the van portion and the passenger communication cord and valve was not in working order when their inspector made a visit to the line in September 1939. Orders were then given for the brake equipment to be repaired.

In 1942 it was decided that this coach could not be classified as a brake van as required by the Ministry of Transport's regulations and an ex-GER bogie brake composite, LNER No. 42871, was sent from Lincoln to Chathill for use as a brake van. The saloon was then used as an ordinary coach until late 1943 when it was sent to Walkergate for overhaul. The vehicle was altered to bring it into line with the Ministry of Transport's regulations for brake vans and the van portion was carried further into the coach resulting in a reduction of seating capacity. The tables were removed, also the roof openings for the gas lamps were covered over. To complete the job the coach was repainted a mid-brown and lettered NSR No. 3 in shaded yellow letters whilst the passenger door carried a large yellow shaded figure 2 and the van door was marked "Guard" in a similar style. At this

The ex-NER 5-compartment third coach at Seahouses in June 1934.

H.C. Casserley

The saloon coach converted to a brake, also seen in June 1934.   *H.C. Casserley*

The other side of the saloon coach, after conversion. *H.N. James*

The saloon coach seen here towards the last days of service. *Author*

The three coaches in Watts Hardy's yard, Howdon, after withdrawal. *Left to right*: No. 2, No. 1, No. 3.   *Author*

The GER brake and third coach derelict, after serving as a greenhouse.
Author

LNER 'Y7' locomotive No. 8089 running in to Seahouses station platform. The goods vehicles, uncoupled from the train whilst moving forward, are rolling in to the goods yard. *W.H. Tate*

The velocipede and "trailer". *L.G. Charlton*

time the vacuum brake equipment was reconditioned and a guard's valve fitted into the van portion.

In 1946 the coach again visited the Walkergate shops where oil lighting was fitted, lamps being hung from the roof. This did not prove satisfactory and eventually an oil lamp was fastened to the van partition. A small stove was fitted in the van section by the guard to provide some warmth in the long winter days. In this form the saloon continued in service until the railway closed, and, after standing in the bay at Chathill for some months, it was sold to Watts Hardy & Co., Howdon-on-Tyne, who scrapped it in their yard.

With the withdrawal of most of the air-braked rolling stock in the North Eastern Area of the LNER the latter company could not hire out coaching stock to the NSR from the beginning of 1937. This meant that through excursions ceased and the NSR had to provide more stock for peak loading seasons. In July of that year Mr Meyer journeyed to Stratford to inspect three six-wheeled thirds of Great Eastern design which were offered for sale at £65 each. Two were six-compartment thirds, No. 60883 which was air-braked only, and No. 60916 which was dual fitted. The third vehicle was a brake third, No. 62305 which was dual fitted. Oil lighting was installed in all the vehicles and they entered NSR service still retaining their LNER livery and lettering. The two thirds were considered as replacements for worn-out stock that had been scrapped (the NER compartment and birdcage coaches), whilst the third vehicle was to be an extra brake van. Meyer's system of electric lighting was fitted to No. 62305 but she proved to be a bad riding coach and in 1939 was withdrawn – the body was sold to a Newcastle potato merchant who placed it in a field at North Sunderland, and converted it to a greenhouse. The chassis was scrapped although one wheel set was retained for use on one of the other coaches.

Decorated with maps of the former Great Eastern Railway these coaches carried many hundreds of passengers along the railway but apparently their safety was not all it should be. In 1939 it was reported that the air brake was not working on No. 60883 and the passenger communication apparatus was out of order on No. 60916. These faults were corrected by the end of 1939 and the two coaches were used until 1943 when No. 60883 went to Walkergate for overhaul including the fitting of a through vacuum pipe and repainting in the same style as the saloon. Returned to Chathill in December of that year and renumbered NSR 1, two compartments were branded second class. It was intended to sell No. 60916 and a representative of the Harton Coal Company inspected it but decided the NSR was asking too much money for it. The LNER also intimated that they did not wish to continue the loan of their vehicles so No. 60916 followed its running mates to Walkergate in 1944 where it was overhauled and renumbered NSR 2. Following complaints that no first class accommodation was provided on the NSR this coach was returned with two compartments branded first. At Seahouses, doors were exchanged between the two coaches so that each had one first, one second and four third class compartments. The large figure 1, featured on first class compartment windows by the LNER at that time, was introduced on the NSR at that period.

No lighting was installed in the coaches during the war and, following complaints from regular passengers, the coaches were fitted for oil lights at Walkergate in 1946. In 1949 these were removed and from then on no lighting was provided in these two coaches. Coach No. 2 was involved in an accident in Seahouses yard in 1949, and was then placed in the end of the warehouse road at Seahouses so recently occupied by *Bamburgh.*

Upon closure of the line the two six-wheelers were sold to Watts Hardy & Co. along with the saloon, after resting in the bay at Chathill for some time. They were then taken to Howdon and, after gutting and rebuilding, were sold to the NCB for use on the South Shields, Marsden and Whitburn Colliery railway until that passenger service was withdrawn.

The first LNER vehicle loaned for use as a brake van was an ex-Great Eastern 45 ft bogie brake composite and for a while was joined on the NSR by an ex-NB first, third lavatory composite. This was the only time such a convenience was provided on the railway although it was not available for use. The GE coach, LNER No. 42871, arrived at Chathill on 14th August, 1942 and after staff instruction in the use of the brakes, it went into service until February 1944. It was realised by the management that by using the bogie coach as a brake van they were hauling a lot of dead weight, so the LNER was approached in 1942 for the loan of a 10 ton brake van. By 1st December of that year an ex-North British four-wheeled brake van, painted red oxide and without any lettering or builders' plates etc., turned up on the line. Used on the end of mixed trains and fish trains, the van was on loan to the line until closure when it was sent to Walkergate shops for scrapping. The van was handbraked only. Several times throughout the railway's history coaches had to be hired from the North Eastern Railway and its successor whilst repairs were carried out on its own stock. This explains why several pictures of the train show vehicles not described in this section.

Chapter Eight
Signalling, Train Services and Tickets

SIGNALLING

Following the successful application for a Light Railway Order, the North Sunderland Railway was relieved of the obligation to provide signals and the only ones installed were ground signals connected to the catch points at Seahouses. At the Chathill end of the line the NER provided signal protection for their lines within the station limits.

No private telephone system was provided, communication between Seahouses and Chathill was by the GPO network.

Points along the railway were worked from ground frames freed by the Annett's key attached to the single line token. In 1933 it was brought to the Board's notice that the system had fallen into disuse and the dangers arising therefrom were realised; its reinstatement was given priority and by 1934 the key was back in use.

An undertaking was given to the Board of Trade that the line would be worked on the One Engine in Steam (or two locomotives coupled) principle. However, during World War II two locomotives were in use – one on line service and the other shunting at Seahouses. On occasions a fish special preceded the afternoon train to Chathill. The LNER drew up operating rules to cover this type of working.

Limit of shunt boards, mile posts, gradient boards and whistle boards were installed along the line.

The only signal actually on NSR land was the fixed distant at the Seahouses end of the Long Nanny Burn loop. This was to remind the driver to bring his train under control as he was approaching the signalled station at Chathill.

A single line token, cast in gunmetal and stamped "Chathill and Seahouses" was introduced under LNER auspices. A large ring through one end carried the Annett's key.

TRAIN SERVICES

Throughout the negotiations with the contractors before the construction of the railway the Directors kept in touch with the North Eastern management over train services. It was decided by the latter authorities to stop fast trains at Chathill to give early and late connections from both Newcastle and Berwick to Seahouses, additionally the normal local train service would continue to call. The first timetable was drawn up by the Directors on 4th July, 1898 and provided for seven trains each way on weekdays only. Full details of this timetable are given in *Appendix 3*. Journey time was given as 15 minutes, the first train left Seahouses at 7.30 am and the last train was due in at 9.05 pm – if the main line train was late the NSR always waited for it.

Chathill and Seahouses.] 692 **[Newcastle and Sunderland.**

	CHATHILL and SEAHOUSES.—North Sunderland.										
	Down.	**Week Days.**						**Up.**	**Week Days.**		
Miles		gov	mrn	aft	aft	aft	aft		gov	mrn	aft	aft	aft	aft	aft
	Chathill ......dep.	8 20	1020	1 30	3 45	5 15	6 55	....	....	Seahouses.........dep.	7 40	9 35	1 0	2 47	3 e 0	4 45	5 45	....	....
4	Seahouses.....arr.	8 35	1035	1 45	4 0	5 30	7 10	....	4	Chathill 690, 691 arr.	7 55	9 50	1 15	3 s 23	3 15	5 0	6 0	....	....

e Except Saturdays. *s* Saturdays only.

Bradshaw's Passenger Timetable for April 1910.

	CHATHILL and SEAHOUSES.—North Sunderland.										
	Down.	**Week Days only.**						**Up.**	**Week Days only.**		
Miles		gov	mrn	aft	aft	aft			Miles		gov	mrn	aft	aft	aft	aft
	Chathill ....dep.	8 12	10 50	1240	2 0	5 42	7 0	....	Seahouses ....dep.	7 35	9 40	1210	1 15	4 15	6 30	....
4	Seahouses ....arr.	8 27	11 5	1255	2 15	5 57	7 15	....	4	Chathill 734, 735 ...arr.	7 50	9 55	1225	1 30	4 30	6 45	....

Bradshaw's Passenger Timetable for July 1922.

CHATHILL and SEAHOUSES.—North Sunderland.—4 miles. (Time on Journey 15 mins.).
Chathill to Seahouses.   WEEK DAYS at 8 14 & 10 48 mrn. ; 1 45, 5 42. & 6 50 aft.
Trains call at North Sunderland 12 mins. after leaving Chathill.
Seahouses to Chathill.   WEEK DAYS at 7 48 & 9 20 mrn. ; 1 0, 4 10, & 6 20 aft.
Trains call at North Sunderland 3 mins. after leaving Seahouses.

Passenger Timetable for March 1938.

Table 166   **CHATHILL and SEAHOUSES—(North Sunderland Railway)**

Miles		**Week Days only**							Miles		**Week Days only**					
		mrn	mrn		aft	aft	aft				mrn	mrn		aft	aft	aft
	Chathill .... dep	8 50	1050	..	1 45	5 10	6 55	..		Seahouses .... dep	7 40	1015	..	1 5	3 45	6 10
	North Sunderland	9 7	11 7	..	2 2	5 27	7 19	..		North Sunderland	7 43	1018	..	1 8	3 48	6 13
4	Seahouses .... arr	9 10	1110	..	2 5	5 0	7 22	..	4	Chathill .... arr	8 0	1035	..	1 25	4 5	6 30

Passenger Timetable for May 1943.

Table 166   **CHATHILL and SEAHOUSES—(North Sunderland Railway)**

Miles		**Week Days only**							Miles		**Week Days only**							
		mrn	mrn	mrn		aft	aft	aft			mrn	mrn	mrn	**H**	**N**	aft	aft
	Chathill .... dep	8 10	9 35	1050	..	1 45	5 10	6 55		Seahouses .... dep	7 35	9 3	1013	1233	1 8	3 48	6 12
	North Sunderland	8 27	9 52	11 7	..	2 2	5 27	7 12		North Sunderland	7 38		1013	1233	1 8	3 48	6 12
4	Seahouses .... arr	8 30	9 55	1110	..	2 5	5 30	7 15	4	Chathill .... arr	7 55	9 20	1030	1250	1 25	4 2	6 30

H Mondays and Saturdays. **N** Except Mondays and Saturdays.

Passenger Timetable for May 1946.

Table 166   **CHATHILL and SEAHOUSES—(North Sunderland Railway)**

Miles		**Week Days only**							Miles		**Week Days only**						
		mrn	mrn	mrn		aft	aft				mrn	mrn	mrn		aft	aft	
	Chathill .... dep	8 10	9 35	1050	..	1 45	5 30	6 55		Seahouses .... dep	7 35	8 55	1010		1230	4 0	6 10	..
	North Sunderland	8 27	9 52	11 7	..	2 2	5 47	7 12		North Sunderland	7 38	8 59	1013		1233	4 3	6 13	..
4	Seahouses .... arr	8 30	9 55	1110	..	2 5	5 50	7 15	4	Chathill .... arr	7 55	9 12	1030		1250	4 20	6 30	..

Passenger Timetable for October 1946.

Fares were fixed in the Act of 1892 and confirmed in the Act of 1898 as follows:

First Class   – a maximum of 3*d*. per mile
Second Class – a maximum of 2*d*. per mile
Third Class   – a maximum of 1*d*. per mile

These fares were revised from time to time in line with those charged by the main railway lines and in 1951 the charge for a second class journey between Seahouses and Chathill was 1*s*. 2*d*. single. Travellers upon the railway were permitted to take with them their personal luggage (not exceeding 120 pounds weight if third class tickets were held) without any charge being made.

By arrangement with the North Eastern Railway through excursions were worked and one in 1900 is stated to have consisted of 12 coaches conveying some 280 people. Other trains were advertised in the local press and were not so large. Through excursions were run at irregular intervals until 1936 after which air-braked main line stock was no longer readily available. From that time, if excursions were run, passengers had to change trains at Chathill.

During the 1914–1918 war the railway was under Government control. Train services were reduced but still made connections with main line trains at Chathill. In 1915 there were four trains a day from Seahouses to Chathill and six in the opposite direction. This is unusual as the train had obviously to make the same number of journeys each way.

In 1938 through connections from Seahouses to London via the "Silver Jubilee" were given in the timetable – a bigger contrast in speed and comfort it is hard to imagine! Again six services a day were run but in the summer months a Sunday service was operated with a late train for Newcastle at 8.20 pm. The Sunday service was first introduced in 1934, the economy of diesel-electric operation must have been the deciding factor.

The NSR published its own timetables until 1939 when it passed into LNER control, thereafter the timetable shared a sheet with the Alnmouth–Alnwick line. In 1939 the state of the track was such that speed reductions were necessary and the journey time was extended to 20 minutes. In 1951 the service was still six trains daily – the Sunday service was not reinstated after the war.

The first train each way was the obligatory "Parliamentary" and third class fares were available. The remaining trains of the day were first and second class only.

The second train of the day from Seahouses was a "mixed" train. The passenger coaches were supposed to run next to the locomotive with the goods vans, the brake van or brake coach bringing up the

NORTH SUNDERLAND RAILWAY.

TIME TABLE

From 14th SEPTEMBER, 1931, to 30th APRIL, 1932.

		A.M.	A.M.	P.M.	P.M.	P.M.					
SEAHOUSES	dep.	*7 33	9 20	1 10	4 10	6 30					
CHATHILL	arr.	7 48	9 35	1 25	4 25	6 45					
		A.M.	A.M.	P.M.	P.M.	P.M.					
CHATHILL	dep.	*8 12	10 48	†2 0	†5 42	†6 55					
SEAHOUSES	arr.	8 27	11 3	2 15	5 57	7 10					

* Third Class (Parliamentary) Train.

† The 9.20 a.m., 12.22, 4.0 and 5.38 p.m. Express Trains from Newcastle stop at Chathill, connections arrive at Seahouses at 11.3 a.m., 2.15, 5.57 and 7.10 p.m.

THROUGH SERVICE.
In connection with L.N.E.R.

			A.M.	A.M.	P.M.	P.M.	E P.M.
Seahouses	-	dep.	7 33	9 20	1 10	4 10	6 30
Chathill -	-	arr.	7 48	9 35	1 25	4 25	6 45
Alnmouth	-	,,	8 32	10 3	2 13	5 22	9 57
Alnwick	-	,,	8 54	10 27	2 43	5 37	10 15
Morpeth	-	,,	9 15	10 29	3 20	6 7	10 27
Newcastle	-	,,	9 45	10 56	3 50	6 39	11 2
Belford -	-	,,	8 18	10 41	1 46	5 28	7 2
Berwick	-	,,	9 0	11 7	2 6	5 50	7 22
				P.M.			
Edinburgh	-	,,		12 42	3 25	8 26	8 42

			A.M.	A.M.	A.M.	P.M.	P.M.
Edinburgh	-	dep.		7 40	10 25	2 35	
Berwick	-	,,	7 23	9 10	1 13	4 54	
Belford -	-	,,	7 56	9 33	1 46	5 27	
Newcastle	-	,,	6 12	9 20	12 22	4 0	5 38
Morpeth	-	,,	6 56	9 49	12 52	4 28	6 9
Alnwick	-	,,	7 20	9 55	1 5	4 48	6 22
Alnmouth	-	,,	7 33	10 19	1 28	5 9	6 35
Chathill	-	,,	8 12	10 48	2 0	5 42	6 55
Seahouses	-	arr.	8 27	11 3	2 15	5 57	7 10

E—L.N.E.R train from Berwick calls at Chathill at 9.42 p.m. when required.

Fares.

	SINGLE.			RETURN.		
	1st Class.	2nd Class.	3rd Class Parliamentary	1st Class.	2nd Class.	3rd Class Parliamentary
	s. d.	s. d.	s. d.	s. d.	s. d.	s. d.
Seahouses to Chathill -	1 2	0 11	0 9	2 4	1 10	1 6

Through Tickets

From Seahouses to:—	Experimental Fares		SINGLE.		RETURN.	
	3rd Class SINGLE.	3rd Class RETURN.	1st Class	2nd Class to Chathill, 3rd beyond.	1st Class	2nd Class to Chathill, 3rd beyond.
	s. d.	s. d.	s. d.	s. d.	s. d.	s. d.
Alnmouth	2 2	3 10	3 7	2 5	7 2	4 10
Alnwick -	2 3	3 10	4 3	2 9	8 6	5 6
Belford -			2 5	1 8	4 10	3 4
Berwick -		•3 7	5 7	3 7	11 2	7 2
Heaton -			10 6	6 6	21 0	13 0
Newcastle		•6 9	10 11	6 9	21 10	13 6
Tweedmouth			5 4	3 5	10 8	6 10
Monkseaton (via Hartley)			10 1	6 8	20 2	12 6
Monkseaton (via Heaton)			12 2	7 6	24 4	15 0
Wallsend (via Heaton)			10 11	6 9	21 10	13 6
Tyne Dock and South Shields			13 1	8 1	26 2	16 2

* Cheap tickets Thursdays and Saturdays, single fare for double journey.

PERIODICAL OR SEASON TICKETS.
SEAHOUSES TO CHATHILL.

12 MONTHS.		6 MONTHS.		3 MONTHS.		2 MONTHS.		1 MONTH.		14 DAYS.	
1st Class.	2nd Class.	1st Class.	2nd Class.	1st Class.	2nd Class.	1st Class.	2nd Class.	1st Class.	2nd Class.	1st Class.	2nd Class.
£ s. d.	£ s. d.	£ s. d.	£ s. d.	£ s. d.	£ s. d.	£ s. d.	£ s. d.	£ s. d.	£ s. d.	£ s. d.	£ s. d.
11 12 6	7 14 6	6 7 6	4 5 6	3 9 9	2 6 6	2 10 3	1 13 9	1 11 6	1 1 0	1 0 3	0 13 6

Periodical Tickets are issued at half-price to children under 15 years of age, and also to scholars, students, and apprentices learning a profession or trade, and not in receipt of salary, up to 18 years of age, on production by them of a Certificate from the Master of the School, the Principal of the College, or their Employer, as the case may be. A deposit of 5s. is required in respect of Periodical Tickets taken for a period of less than 3 months, such deposit will be returned to the Ticket Holder provided the ticket be given up on expiry.

The issuing of Tickets to Passengers to places off this Company's line is an arrangement made for the greater convenience of the public; but the Company will not be held responsible for the non-arrival of this Company's own trains in time for any nominally corresponding train on the London & North Eastern Company's line, nor for any delay, detention, or other loss or injury whatsoever which may arise therefrom, or for the acts or defaults of other parties, nor for the correctness of the times over the London & North Eastern Company's line.

PARCELS sent by Passenger Trains are received by the Company to be carried only on the same conditions relative to the times of the trains as stated in the notice above given.

N.B.—The hours or times stated in these Tables are appointed as those at which it is intended, as far as circumstances will permit, the Passenger Trains should depart from and arrive at Seahouses and Chathill respectively, but their departure or arrival at the times stated is not guaranteed, nor will the Company, under any circumstances, be held responsible for delay or detention, however occasioned, or any consequences arising therefrom.

61, Westgate Road, Newcastle-on-Tyne,
14th September, 1931.

RICHARD SMITH, Secretary.

JOHN BELL & CO., Printers, Railway Lane, Pilgrim Street, Newcastle.

A typical NSR Public Timetable sheet. These were well distributed locally, in shops, etc.
Author

rear. In practice this did not always work out as planned and over the years the wagons ran next to the locomotive and the coaches were at the rear – all right if the wagons were braked so enabling a continuous brake to be in operation. In 1936, when only the brake coach was available for traffic, it was impossible to work trains in accordance with the "regulations". The second train of the day from Chathill also was "mixed" and operated in a similar manner.

At Seahouses the fish catch was usually auctioned in the early afternoon and then boxed and prepared for transit on the later after-noon train. The fish wagons, if fitted with brakes that enabled a continuous brake to function on the train, could run between the locomotive and the coaches otherwise a passenger coach was sup-posed to run between the locomotive and them. At Chathill the coaches were placed in the goods sidings. The North Sunderland locomotive drew the fish wagons down the east siding alongside the up main line, and then pushed them up to the back of the Newcastle-bound main line train whilst it was standing at the platform. If the fish landing was heavy or late the fish wagons were be worked to Chathill on the later train and would be left in the east siding. The main line fish train which did not convey passenger carrying stock would then stop clear of the points and back into the siding to pick up the wagons.

The authorised way of working was for the train from Seahouses to run straight into the bay at Chathill. After all the passengers had detrained, the train was to be propelled to the loop where the loco was to run-round then again propel the stock to Chathill where the shunting operations could be started. In his report of 1933 Mr Meyer stated that fly-shunting was now being carried out at Chathill and as far as he could trace no authority for this had been given. By this means operations were speeded up but three people were needed instead of two when running-round, also the practice was dangerous in the dark, frosty, or foggy weather. From then, depending on circumstances, the train was either fly shunted or run-round. Some-times the locomotive ran-round the train before arriving at Chathill, again against regulations.

A Mrs Cuthbertson ran a horse-drawn conveyance between Bam-burgh and Seahouses to connect with the trains, an arrangement made between the railway and her. This connection was shown in the timetable for 1899, and even though it was not a paying proposition it ran until 1st April, 1905 when the proprietor replaced horse traction with a motor car. How long this arrangement lasted is not known but the route was eventually incorporated in the Alnwick–Belford service operated by the United Automobile Services, the local 'bus operator.

In 1934 the LNER motor cartage service was extended to cover the

NSR and a lorry used to journey from Belford to Seahouses then load up and deliver on behalf of the NSR. When the locomotive was out of service and no spare power was available the railway hired one of Beecroft's taxis and it ran between Seahouses and Chathill calling at North Sunderland at train times. This was necessary as the NSR had a contract with the GPO for carrying mails (it is of interest that the UAS bus dealt with this traffic after closure). Fish was carried on a hired lorry to Chathill and the LNER lorry started its journey from Chathill on such occasions.

Whilst the quarry was in operation rail traffic was operated by the NSR. The Board realised that danger might result to their locomotive running right into the quarry and it was agreed that the loco would run onto the tangent track, the wagons would be man-handled into position, later to be pushed out and hauled to Chathill.

Coal sales at Seahouses were carried out by the railway, the station master acting as agent and receiving a commission on sales. The practice of coal sales from station yards was peculiar to the North Eastern Railway but at least one attempt to break the monopoly occurred in 1922. The NSR minutes recorded that, as a result of Shilbottle Colliery having been purchased by the Co-operative Wholesale Society Ltd, the Seahouses Co-operative Society demanded selling rights. A 50-50 settlement was reached but no space was allotted to the Co-operative Society in Seahouses station yard.

Incoming traffic at Seahouses was mainly coal and salt whilst fish was the principal outgoing traffic. Special fish trains commenced in 1943 requiring the use of two locomotives on the line. It was recorded that in 1949, with only one locomotive in use, some 71 such trains were run between April and September.

When extra passenger trains were run at weekends or holiday periods chalked notices were placed around the village; regular time-tables were displayed in shop windows, etc.

TICKETS

Tickets issued by the NSR were a multi-coloured assortment, a different colour for each class and type of ticket. Headed North Sunderland Railway or NSR, they were printed by the NER who also supplied stores, stationery, and forms for monthly statements similar to those used on their own stations. One batch of NSR tickets was in fact headed NER. Tickets were issued for first, second and third class, and second class tickets to stations off the line were marked "Second class to Chathill, third class beyond". Similarly main line tickets were marked "Third class to Chathill, second class on NSR". At Chathill, where tickets were issued in the main line booking office, they carried

The "crew" posing alongside a well turned out No. 68089 at Seahouses.

Author's Collection

Bamburgh at Seahouses with three Highland coaches on 8th October, 1900. This is one of only two known photographs showing the Highland coaches in use.

Ken Nunn

The Lady Armstrong in the fish dock siding at Seahouses. Part of the diesel
engine casing is removed to assist cooling on a hot day in July 1946.

L.G. *Charlton*

Bamburgh shunting at Seahouses in 1932.

L.G. *Charlton*

LNER No. 986 seen here at Seahouses Yard with a diesel on a passenger train
(*left*) and the NB brake (*right*).   *Author's Collection*

LNER No. 2209 in very clean condition pulls away from Chathill with a fish
train for the south. The NSR's birdcage brake is standing in the goods yard.
L.G. Charlton

Class 'Y7' No. 68089 has just arrived at Chathill with the morning mixed train. Note that unbraked wagons are running between the locomotive and the passenger coaches. *Author's Collection*

Chathill station. "The Farne Islander" has arrived with Class 'Y7' No. 68089 in charge. Between the locomotive and the coaches are vacuum braked fish vans. Note the mix of timber and concrete sleepers in both platform and goods road. The cabin built over the sidings ground frame is also evident.

N. Stead

the main line railway's title. Season tickets were available on the NSR whilst the Directors had their own "fold-over" tickets. Special fish workers' tickets were issued in the season. Third class or Parliamentary fares were only issued on the first train of the day each way to meet the requirements of the law.

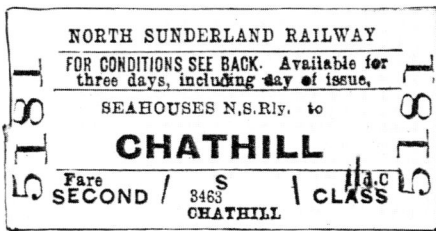

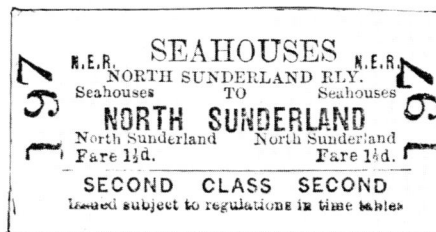

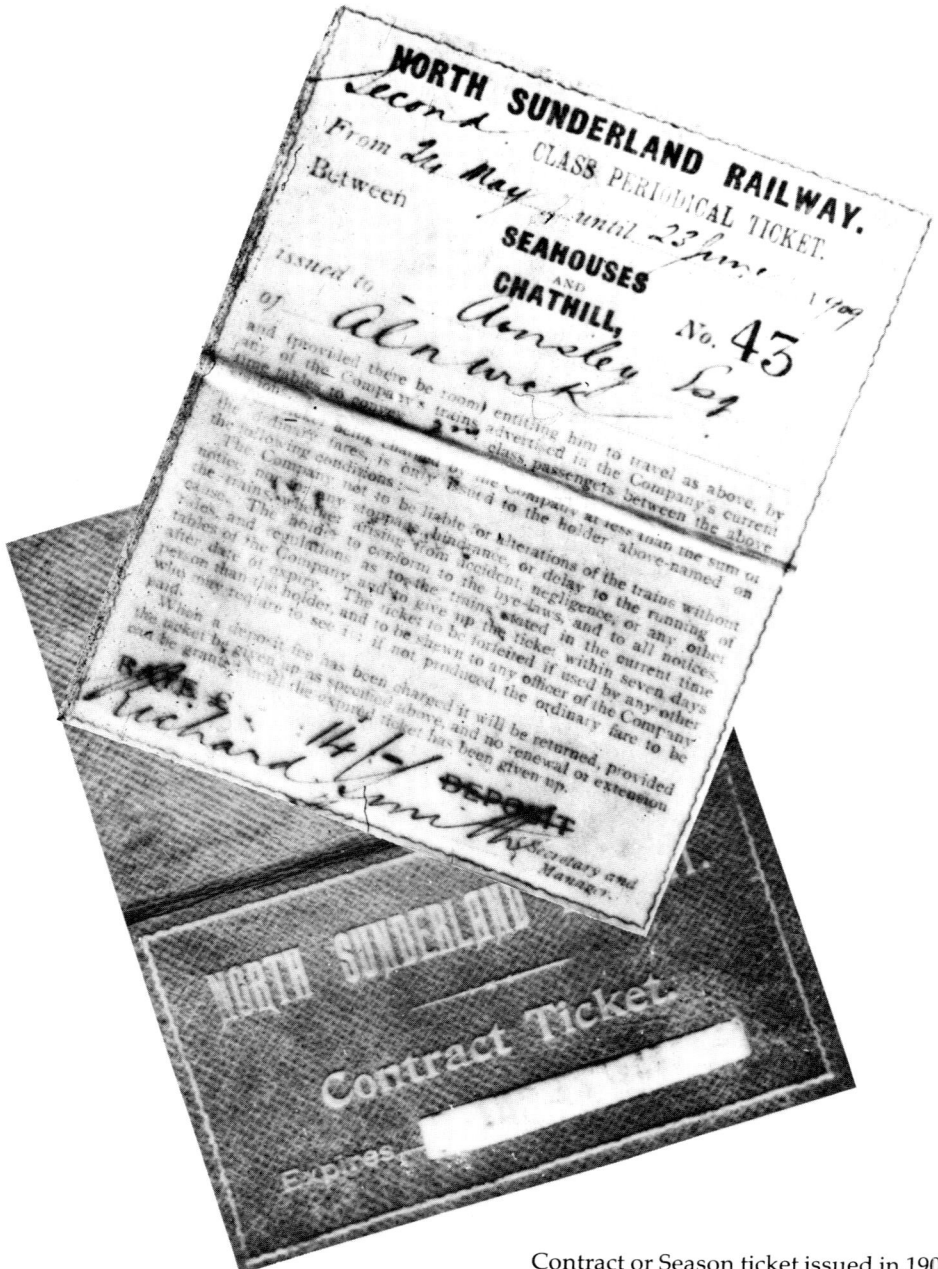

Contract or Season ticket issued in 1909.

Chapter Nine
Operations

In *Chapter 2* the events which led to the building of the railway have been recorded, however by the end of 1898 the Company was not financially clear.

The Directors in their search for capital to pay the contractor decided to ask Lord Armstrong if he would increase his subscription but he declined to do so. As a result Mr Meyer was asked to explain the financial situation to Whitakers. The coaches so recently bought were mortgaged to raise more money and when the facts were put to the contractors they asked to be relieved of the 12 months' guaranteed maintenance. This the Directors refused to agree to.

The newly-appointed station master, Mr English, asked the Board to build him a house on spare land they owned in Seahouses, but they decided to find out if a building society would help in the matter. Eventually it was agreed to raise his salary to help pay for lodgings.

Uniforms for the staff were provided in 1899 and were very similar to those worn by the North Eastern uniformed personnel; in later days NER and LNER uniforms were issued but with NSR lettering.

The following year saw an agreement with the Duke of Northumberland who had wanted a bridge building across the railway at the Long Nanny Burn; the need for this is obscure but negotiations over it were prolonged. In the same year an agreement was made with the NER over the display of posters and McCorquodales printed some illustrated ones featuring the Longstone Lighthouse, the one-time home of Grace Darling, from which she set out to rescue the passengers and crew of the stricken *Forfarshire* that wild night in September 1838. Drainage works, including the laying of additional pipes, were found necessary in Chathill cutting – more expense. However, the Board was feeling optimistic and a statement from a "Company's official" published in the April 1901 issue of *The Locomotive* stated that if traffic continued to develop at the present rate a second locomotive would soon be needed! The plan to lay out land at Monks House as a development area to be known as St-Aidans-by-the-Sea was also revealed; this was perhaps to justify the capital raised for building the extension but spent on the original line.

The same issue of *The Locomotive* noted that through excursions from Newcastle to Seahouses had been operated in 1900, using NER stock throughout but with the NSR locomotive between Chathill and Seahouses. The *Newcastle Daily Chronicle* carried an advert for an excursion to Seahouses on Wednesday 13th June, 1900 leaving Newcastle at 12.00 noon.

In 1901 proposals were put forward to build a raised coal drop at Seahouses so that standard North Eastern bottom door wagons could be unloaded but the estimated cost of £500 was too much for the Board. If such a scheme had been carried out the whole appearance of the goods yard would have been altered. Mr Meyer suggested to the Board at the end of the year that if the North Sunderland station building was made into a dwelling for the guard, his wife could act as crossing keeper. After ascertaining that this was in order with the Board of Trade a local builder was engaged to alter the station building and to make a small extension to it. At the same time Seahouses engine shed was altered.

The management faced an unusual problem in 1903 – two men travelled from Chathill to North Sunderland without paying a fare and when challenged by the guard they refused to pay. The guard took their names and addresses but, in spite of long discussion, the Directors could not decide on what course of action to take so eventually they wrote to other railway companies to see what they did in similar circumstances. In later years those caught travelling without a ticket and refusing to pay the fare were taken to court.

Bamburgh was finally paid for in August 1905 and the Board decided to exercise their option to buy the locomotive outright for one shilling; the coaches were similarly paid for the following year.

Passenger traffic was obviously not fulfilling expectations because in 1907 three coaches were overhauled and repainted whilst the remaining two were converted to wagons for internal stone traffic.

About the same time a meeting was held with Mr Thwaite, the quarry master at Pasture Hill, and an agreement was entered into regarding the working of stone traffic. Some 20 chains of track were laid from the NSR to the quarry and the company's locomotive worked there but wagons were manhandled within the quarry. By 1912 the quarry was not a success, the stone was of a poor quality and the various railway companies were not offering low enough rates for the owner to send it to Scotland as intended. The Board of the NSR was very sympathetic and reduced their rates in an attempt to help but within a short space of time the quarry closed.

The railway's affairs jogged along quietly for the next few years. The Company, whilst not paying dividends, did at least manage to stay solvent; however, in 1911 it was informed that the signalling at Chathill was in a very poor state and needed renewal. The Board was not over-cheerful to hear that the passenger traffic was declining due to the increase in the number of motor cars in the district but agreed to pay for the necessary work to be carried out by the North Eastern Railway.

Clouds of war were gathering over Europe and with the declaration of hostilities in 1914 the NSR, complete with its one locomotive and two coaches, passed into Government control. All earnings etc. were based on the 1913 figures whilst the staff received war bonuses as increases in salary. Train services were reduced and mixed trains were introduced from this period, possibly in a move to save coal. The original station master, Mr English, resigned his post in 1913 before emigrating to Rhodesia and Mr J. Cuthbertson, who had joined the railway in 1900 as a boy, was appointed to the post. In his first years of control, several far-reaching practices were started, practices which took a lot of breaking and which were conveniently blamed on the war years.

At the end of the hostilities *Bamburgh* was in poor shape and was sent to the Leeds works of its makers for heavy overhaul, this being paid for by the Government. When the two coaches were reported unsafe by an NER inspector in 1921 the Board argued that as they were in sound order when they were taken over then the Government should return them in a like condition. Unfortunately this did not work out and the NSR had to pay for repairs at Walkergate shops. The job was delayed through the coal stoppage and, when the bills for the hire of two NER coaches and the repair to their own arrived, the NSR sought to have the hire bill reduced by the amount of time delay attributable to the coal stoppage – again without success.

At busy times, such as Newcastle's Race Week holiday, the railway hired extra rolling stock from the NER or its successor, the LNER, so to avoid this in 1924 a saloon coach was purchased from Watts Hardy & Co. of Howdon on Tyne, and with three coaches all traffic presenting itself was catered for during the next few years.

That the locomotive was not receiving proper maintenance in the ensuing period is made obvious by the need for very heavy repairs, this time at Gateshead in 1926 following an inspector's report that it was not safe to run.

Their own locomotive returned to the NSR on 2nd October and, so refurbished, it again started to work the services. The track was also not receiving proper maintenance and in 1927 a goods train was derailed in the cutting. The NER inspector reported the cause to be the track spreading on rotten sleepers. A limited amount of interest was being shown by the Board in their property because tenders were invited for painting the buildings and coaches. It was stated that, following the period of government control, operating costs had increased. This is made obvious in reference to wages in the minutes – talk was made of reducing wages, and when an employee retired the person engaged in his place received a considerably smaller wage.

Being slow to pay its accounts with the NER and later the LNER, there were rumours concerning a "take over" by the LNER. That railway's inspectors visited the line and presented lengthy reports on the North Sunderland's condition and prospects, but all came to nought. The NSR management kept up a running battle with the LNER over their share of through rates and in due course the latter company threatened to withdraw through working and booking facilities unless payments were made.

In 1933 the Board of the NSR agreed to the appointment of Mr Meyer as General Manager to take charge of the engineering and operating side of the railway's affairs. Until that time the railway had been administered by the Secretary under direct orders from the Board. Meyer presented a report to the Board in the May – and what a state the railway was in! The track was overgrown and the Long Nanny loop was virtually impassable, in fact the sale of the rails was suggested. The locomotive was in need of boiler repairs and the coaching stock required renewal. The Annett's key system of point operation had been abandoned by the men and was now in a very bad state. In his opinion it was absolutely necessary and should never have been allowed to fall into disuse. Fly shunting was carried out at Chathill and he could not find out on whose authority it had been started.

He continued that it had been necessary to hire an LNER locomotive due to the appalling state of *Bamburgh* but he was hoping to secure on loan a diesel electric locomotive from Armstrong Whitworths. This would cost £8 per week but he felt that, in view of the advertising potential and valuable operating experience the makers would gain, they should lend it free – if not indeed present it to the railway. This was probably said because Lord Armstrong was in the chair, if so, it fell on closed ears! The diesel worked the train for some six months – no continuous brake was fitted to the locomotive. He also said that as the journey of 4¼ miles was so short consideration should be given to single manning the steam locomotive. The daily mileage for *Bamburgh* was only 42 [sic].

At this time *Bamburgh* was being repaired by a local man at North Sunderland. With the demonstrator diesel proving successful the Company went ahead and purchased their second locomotive in 1934, *The Lady Armstrong*. Publicity issued by Armstrong Whitworths at the time made great play of the statement that steam had been completely superseded by diesel!

The following year Meyer informed the Board that the Annett's key working had been re-introduced, gradient and mile posts were being restored, and the bridges repaired and painted. Following the acquisition of the diesel electric locomotive the water tower at Long Nanny Burn was to be converted to store oil with a pump to discharge rail wagons into it. The saloon coach had very satisfactorily been made into a brake second by transferring the hand brake from the old coach, and it had also been fitted with electric light worked from the diesel loco generator. The track had been cleaned up and the loop was back in use. *Bamburgh*, following her repairs, was now available for sale or as a stand-by locomotive. The Board fortunately did not decide to sell. In connection with the LNER a Sunday service was worked in the summer months with excursion bookings (half day) from Newcastle, passengers having to change at Chathill.

With the use of a diesel locomotive it was possible to reduce the staff level. However, if *Bamburgh* was steamed there was a shuffle of personnel. The guard, being the senior employee, drove the steam locomotive with the regular diesel locomotive driver firing for him. The leading platelayer became the train guard for the time.

In 1937 three coaches were bought from the LNER and, apart from fitting the brake third with electric light, little work was done to them. The brake third was found to be prone to derailments and was withdrawn by mid-1939 and the body sold. The intention had been to run the three coaches as a high capacity train at holiday periods and for the rest of the year the brake third would suffice.

Mr Meyer's hopes for economy with a diesel locomotive were shattered in 1938 when the locomotive failed at least twice with a broken crankshaft, so once more the steam engine came back into its own. Meanwhile, the debt to the LNER was increasing and in January 1939, an investigation into the finances of the NSR was made by Messrs Peat, Marwick, Mitchell & Co. As a result of the position disclosed, and with a view to the most economical working possible, an agreement was made between the LNER and the NSR which provided, amongst others, that a nominee of the LNER should re-place the manager of the NSR. The agreement provided that:

a) The LNER's district goods manager at Newcastle, or any other officer that the LNER may nominate at any future date should, with the approval of the NSR Board, act as manager of the NSR, which would pay the LNER an acknowledgement of £10 per annum in respect of management.

b) Similarly the LNER's revenue accountant at Newcastle, or any other officer, should act as Secretary and accountant of the NSR without charge.

c) The LNER's accountant shall audit the NSR's accounts without charge.

d) The NSR's Directors' fees to be waived.

e) The proceeds of coal sale at Seahouses to continue to be regarded as part of the NSR's revenue.

f) The agreement to be the subject of termination by either side giving six months' notice in writing.

Up to 1939 losses on the working of the NSR were charged to a general reserve, but by that date the fund was exhausted. The line therefore passed into the control of the LNER who were, in 1940, instructed by the Ministry of Transport to operate it through special provisions in the Control Nett Revenue Account.

Once they had settled in, and following the upsets due to the outbreak of World War II, the new management started to examine the railway. Great concern was felt over the mode of operation and the signal inspectors and rolling stock people all made their reports so that precise operating instructions could be drawn up.

The first action was to reduce the speed limit to 15 miles per hour because of track conditions. An inspector then reported that the Annett's key which locked the fouling points at Chathill and Sea-houses was carried by the guard and not on the locomotive. (This was probably a convenience due to the single manning of the diesel locomotive.) Trains were run loose coupled with the brake saloon at the Seahouses end thus infringing the Board of Trade regulations. In any case it was doubtful if the brake would be sufficiently powerful to hold the train in the event of a runaway.

The compressor on the steam locomotive did not work, the saloon brake did not have an air brake cock in the van and the passenger communication cord was not in use. One six-wheeled coach was air braked only but the system did not work. The other three coaches were dual fitted but only one had a working vacuum brake. This vehicle was electrically lit but was not used due to frequent derail-ments. It was suggested that the Westinghouse brake be repaired on an urgent basis. The NSR's coaches were sufficient for the traffic presented except in the Newcastle Race Week when two or three coaches were hired from the LNER and trains were worked double-headed.

The continuous brake was brought back into full working order by the end of 1939, but it was not until 1942 that precise operating instructions were laid down.

In that year the inspector reported that on down trains to Sea-houses the air brake was worked and up to six wagons were hauled as a tail load. On trains from Seahouses wagons were placed between the locomotive and the coaches therefore the continuous brake was inoperative. Passengers were consequently being carried in unbraked vehicles, again infringing the Board of Trade requirements. Immedi-ately instructions were given to the station master that on no account must passengers be carried in unbraked vehicles and that in future coaches must run next to the locomotive for both journeys.

It appears that this practice stemmed from the days of World War I and that it took a lot of stopping is obvious from the number of letters the management wrote to the station master on this subject.

The following month Cuthbertson was told to instruct the guard that a tail lamp must be carried on the last vehicle of all trains run over the line and to tell the locomotive crew that when waiting at Chathill between trains they had to carry out any shunting that the station master there may require. The NSR locomotive was not, however, to operate on LNER track.

In 1942 a carriage and wagon inspector made a journey to Seahouses from Walkergate to see the saloon brake and in his report he stated that it could not be classified as a brake van within the Ministry of Transport's requirements. The passenger communication system was inoperative through pipes being blanked off following corrosion and there still was no brake cock in the guard's compartment.

Upon the realisation that the saloon brake was not a satisfactory vehicle, the LNER arranged for a brake composite, dual fitted, to be transferred from Lincoln, and by mid-August 1942 the NSR staff had been instructed how to use it and it was then employed as a brake van. Meanwhile a 10 ton goods van was sought – it would not be so long and was only half the weight of the coach. On 14th November an un-numbered and unlettered ex-North British Railway brake van was delivered on loan from the LNER.

In the September of 1942 a signalling inspector was asked to make a report on the railway so that a set of operating rules could be drawn up and issued to the staff. He stated that only one employee had passed the LNER eyesight test and that none had had a medical examination. He also stated that a single line staff, lettered "Seahouses–Chathill", should be provided to which the Annett's key should be fixed. No signals, lamps or discs were provided on the level crossing gates at North Sunderland and it was essential that this was remedied, especially before the winter nights came. Mixed trains were permissible providing no more than six loaded or nine empty wagons were hauled and that the passengers were in a braked coach. A tail load of one vehicle (unbraked) was to be allowed between Chathill and Seahouses, but not in the reverse direction.

Also in 1942 a proposal was put to the management to change the name of the railway to the Seahouses Railway, a title which would be less cumbersome and not so apt to mislead. This proposal was never acted upon.

LNER track laying gangs moved on to the line in June 1942 and started to lay some 1700 wood sleepers and 500 concrete pots, a number to be increased within the next few years. Locomotive failures increased and at the end of 1942 a non-vacuum braked Sentinel steam loco of LNER class 'Y1' was in use for shunting and hauling goods trains. During its short stay on the line double-manning problems reared their head. The NSR driver would not operate a Sentinel on his own. Experiments with a two speed machine were also dogged by the same problem.

Cuthbertson retired at the beginning of December 1942 with a gratuity – he had not been a member of a pension scheme. The appointment of a new station master was held up because no suitable house was available, so the LNER provided a relief man for a few years.

In 1943 it was decided to make use of the loop at Long Nanny as a store for wagons following an occasion when Seahouses yard was choked with 22 wagons and Chathill had a further 33 for the railway. To use the loop for that purpose trap points were necessary but to save costs swing chocks locked by Annett's key were considered. When the costs of the scheme were gone into it was found cheaper to bring the long siding at North Sunderland back into use. It had been planned to put camping coaches at North Sunderland in 1940 but the war prevented it. The management had had the offer of two Italian Railways ferry vans lying at Tyne Dock in 1943 which they thought were suitable for alteration. No action was taken on the proposal which was a great pity.

The railway's three coaches were sent to LNER's Walkergate shops in 1943 for refurbishing whilst the LNER loaned two bogie coaches to the NSR. Consideration was given to selling one of the ex-Great Eastern vehicles to the Harton Coal Company for use on its passenger trains but the price was too high for them. In any case the LNER wanted the vehicles it had loaned to the NSR back, so all three of them were eventually dealt with and returned to Chathill. It was not until 1944 that the LNER retrieved its rolling stock.

Fish landings continued to be heavy and it was necessary to operate two locomotives on the railway, one shunting at Seahouses and the other working trips. When the NSR's own motive power was in use the diesel worked the passenger trains and the steamer was used for shunting and, when necessary, working special fish trains to Chathill. If only one NSR locomotive was available it worked the passenger trains using the air brake and the LNER locomotive did the shunting. Not until vacuum braked coaches were available could the LNER's engine pull the passenger train. Trouble was experienced over the operating regulations – to perform its work the shunting engine crew needed the single line staff with the key, however, according to the regulations, the trip locomotive crew should carry it. To get around the problem it was proposed to install a signal 80 yards west of the most westerly point at Seahouses connected to the ground frame. On some occasions it was also necessary for the shunting locomotive to work a train to Chathill whilst the passenger train followed. As a temporary expedient a verbal instruction was given to the first driver not to leave Chathill until the second had arrived, then both locomotives were to work back coupled together.

In 1945 operating instructions were at last ready; these stated it was necessary for the station master to obtain the Annett's key from the possession of the chargeman platelayer to unlock the points leading from the single line to the yard if a shunting locomotive was in use. When two trains were to run to Chathill the first driver had to be in possession of a ticket and the second a staff; before starting the return journey they were to confer and the first driver again carry the ticket.

Instead of a signal, a "limit of shunt" board was installed at the proposed position and drivers of incoming trains had to stop if a shunting locomotive was in use and ascertain that the road to the platform was clear.

Following successful trials with a class 'Y7' locomotive the NSR paid for modifications necessary to enable them to hire it for use on all services.

Two coaches were also dual fitted with air and vacuum brake, but coach No. 2 was fitted with a through pipe only and was to be used as a strengthener and did run between the locomotive and coach No. 1. To prevent the paintwork on one side being blistered by the sun it was arranged for the coaches to be turned. In spite of the loan of the 'Y7', on 17th October, 1945 no locomotive was in working order and, as a taxi could not be obtained, twelve passengers had to make their own way to Chathill.

The North Sunderland Railway once again had a station master of its own when, on 1st May, 1945 Mr Pearson, recently demobilised, was appointed following satisfactory reports from the LNER station masters at Belford and Chathill under whom he had trained. Complaints were received by him over the coaches and the lack of lights and they made separate journeys to Walkergate so that oil lamps could be fitted. A further complaint was similar to that received in 1899. Sparks from the locomotive chimney had set fire to a haystack causing £102 worth of damage, consequently a price was obtained for a supply of a spark arrester.

The NSR management, realising that their own two locomotives were nearing the end of their useful lives, asked the LNER to look around for a suitable diesel locomotive. The only solution the LNER could come up with was an offer to rebuild a 'Y7' into an 0–6–0T similar to a 'J79' and sell it to the NSR for £1370. The offer was turned down.

The winter of 1946–1947 was long and cold and the 'Y7', now renumbered 8089, was unable to run a service from 10th to 13th February due to blockage of the line by snow drifts. NSR employees had the line re-opened on 14th February but by the 26th it was blocked again. This time the drifting was worse and it was not until 8th March that the line was once more open, only to be closed for 12

days when on 13th March the level crossing gates at North Sunderland could not be seen under the blanket of snow. The LNER snow-
ploughs were too heavy for the NSR's permanent way so all clearing
had to be done manually.

The LNER cartage service was not quite what it should be and in
February 1947 a three-wheel delivery cycle was borrowed from the
main line company so that parcels arriving after the lorry had gone
could be speedily delivered. In September *Bamburgh* finally came to
the end of its working life and it was put at the end of the warehouse
siding at Seahouses awaiting the Board's decision on its fate. With the
diesel locomotive already at Darlington out of use, the 'Y7' was left in
charge until the autumn of 1948 when it needed urgent workshop
attention. An ex-Lancashire and Yorkshire Railway "Pug" 0–4–0ST
was sent to Seahouses as a substitute but, being unable to handle
passenger trains, did not last long.

With No. 8089 back in harness, the railway settled down to a period
of uneventful operations with only the occasional interruption due to
engine failures. In 1949 the oil lighting was removed from the coaches
– the vibrations caused the lamps to go out and the station master was
very perturbed about the fire hazard.

One of the six-wheelers was derailed in Seahouses yard and was
taken out of service. A fish van was kept coupled to the train for small
loads, the guard objecting to the smell of fish in his van! The remaining two coaches started to show decay and vandals accelerated the
process. Following representations from Pearson the management
refused to consider repairs to the upholstery but did send him a
bundle of old squabs so that he could carry out the necessary work
himself.

A letter from the Railway Executive cancelling the agreement originally drawn up by the LNER and NSR in 1939 was received by the
Board at its meeting on 5th July, 1951 and, as the Board unanimously
agreed that it was impossible for the NSR to run the railway without
Railway Executive aid, it resolved to cease operations as from 27th
October, 1951. So ended railway workings to Seahouses after nearly
53 years of independence, the NSR having been passed by in the
groupings of 1923 and nationalisation of 1948.

Chapter Ten

Accidents

It is very pleasant to record that no fatal accidents occurred on the railway in spite of the state of disrepair the track, locomotives, and rolling stock were allowed to fall into. Accidents did happen; only twelve days after the railway opened for freight working *Bamburgh* was derailed at Chathill when the points were opened under her. The leading axle was twisted and the wheelset had to be returned to Manning Wardle for repair, the NER provided a relief locomotive in the interim.

A field of corn at Fleetham was set on fire the next month and as a result *Bamburgh* was duly fitted with a chimney top spark arrester. In 1905 a goods train was derailed near Chathill causing the cancellation of some passenger trains. The North Eastern inspector reported that "track out of gauge" caused the derailment.

What could have been a serious accident occurred at Seahouses on 14th August, 1924. At that time the Northumberland County Council were carrying out a lot of roadworks in the area and were consigning wagons of tarred stone to North Sunderland. Shunting had been done at North Sunderland and the locomotive started to push four wagons to Seahouses. It was soon realised that the leading three wagons were not coupled to the fourth as, when the locomotive started to brake, the wagons continued to roll, then gathering speed on the down gradient, they careered through the station, crashed through the engine shed and the stone wall, then crossed the Bamburgh road and came to rest in a yard opposite the station. A motor car, driven by a Sunderland doctor, just escaped serious damage. The front and wings were knocked though the driver and his wife (who was riding with him) escaped injury. The NSR paid for the necessary repairs to the car. A few weeks after the accident the doctor reported that his wife was suffering from shock but the Board took no action on his letter.

On 23rd February, 1925 a lady passenger damaged [*sic*] her ankle when alighting from a train at North Sunderland. A claim from her father was probably the driving force in the Board's decision to build a new platform there. Later that year, on 25th November, the engine shed caught fire causing £21 15s. 0d. worth of damage; the locomotive was, however, removed safely.

In a humorous vein – two tup hogs strayed on the line through broken fences or a level crossing gate left open and were killed. £2 10s. 0d. was paid to the farmer as compensation.

These were the nature of the accidents suffered on the line; as time went by the number of derailments increased but, apart from the runaway wagon incident, nothing serious was reported to the Board.

BRITISH RAILWAYS

TRAIN SERVICE
ALNMOUTH and ALNWICK
SEPTEMBER 10th 1951 until further notice

Table 73

WEEKDAYS

London (King's Cross) .... dep	pm 8e20	am 1 0	....		am	am 3 50	am	am 10 5	pm	pm 12 18	....	....	pm 3230	....				
York.................... ,,	1a13	5 4	....		6 40	10 5	11 32	2 p 2	2 50	4 18		....	7 16					
Newcastle............... ,,	3 11	6 52		7 15	9 28	12p21	1Ap20	4 18	5 A 7	6 5	....	....	10 A 0	....				
		am							pm									
Edinburgh .... dep		7 22			6 55	10 25		2 30				8 0						
Berwick .... ,,					8 55	12p11		4 20				9 25						
					SO													
ALNMOUTH............. dep	am 6 30	am 7 42	am 8 30	am 9 0	am 10 25	pm 1 21	pm 2 41	pm 5 23	pm 6 12	pm 7 10	pm 8 45	pm 9 40	pm 10 17	pm 11 27				
ALNWICK .... arr	6 37	7 49	8 37	9 7	10 32	1 28	2 48	5 30	6 19	7 17	8 52	9 47	10 24	11 34				

WEEKDAYS

					SO											
ALNWICK .... dep	am 7 12	am 7a29	am 8 15	am 8 44	am 9 38	am 10a20	pm 12 52	pm 4a25	pm 5 0	pm 6 50	pm 8 25	pm 9 14	pm 10 0	pm 10 0		
ALNMOUTH............. arr	7 18	7 36	8 21	8 50	9 44	10 26	12 58	4 31	5 6	6 56	8 31	9 20	10 6	6 11 6		
		am	am		am	am	pm	pm	pm			pm				
Newcastle .... arr		8 53	9 29		10p45	11 53	2p40	5 57	6 11	....	10s51	11 10				
York................... ,,			11 35		1 31	2 18	4 44		9 16			1 45				
London (King's Cross) .. ,,		2v6	3 29			5 50	9o55		3 a 6			6 5				
	am				am	am		pm	pm							
Berwick .... arr	8 10		10 7		11 7	11 7		2 8	6 25	8w3						
Edinburgh .... ,,	9 26				12 41			3 35	9 t 2	10 0						

A—Through Train between Newcastle and Alnwick   B—Passengers can arrive King's Cross 8.10 pm by Pullman Car train, supplementary charge   E—Also applies on Sunday nights   F—On Saturdays arrives Newcastle 10.50 am   K—On Sundays arrives York 1.11 am   S or SO—Saturdays only   V—By the Tees—Tyne Pullman from Newcastle, Saturdays excepted, supplementary charge.   Z—Except Saturdays passengers can leave King's Cross 4.45 pm by Pullman Car train to Newcastle. Supplementary charge   a—am   d—On Thursdays and Saturdays arrives Newcastle 2.3 pm   f—On Saturdays arrives Edinburgh 9.4 pm   p—pm   w—On Saturdays arrives Berwick 8.6 pm

CHATHILL and SEAHOUSES
(NORTH SUNDERLAND RAILWAY)

Table 75

	WEEKDAYS								WEEKDAYS						
	am	am	am	am	pm	pm	pm			am	am	am	pm	pm	pm
Edinburgh .... dep	....	6 55		10 25	2 30										
Berwick .... ,,	7 22	8 55		12p11	4 20	....	....	SEAHOUSES .... dep	7 35	8 55	10 5	12 15	4 20	6 45	...
Newcastle .... dep		7 15	9 28	12p21	4 18	6 5	....	North Sunderland ...... ,,	7 38	8 58	10 8	12 18	4 23	6 48	...
								CHATHILL............. arr	7 55	9 15	10 25	12 35	4 40	7 5	...
	am	am	am	am	pm	pm	pm		am	am	am	pm	pm	pm	
CHATHILL .... dep	8 10	9 35	10 50	1 40	5 50	7 35	...	Newcastle .... arr	9 29	10e45	....	2b0	6 11	11A10	...
North Sunderland...... ,,	8 27	9 52	11 7	1 57	6 7	7 52	...	Berwick .... arr		10 7	11 7	2 8	6 25	8w3	...
SEAHOUSES .... arr	8 30	9 55	11 10	2 0	6 10	7 55	...	Edinburgh .... ,,			12p41	3 35	9 J 2	10 0	...

A—On Saturdays arrives Newcastle 10.51 pm   B—On Saturdays arrives Berwick 8.6 pm   D—On Thursdays and Saturdays arrives Newcastle 2.3 pm   J—On Saturdays arrives Edinburgh 9.4 pm   K—On Saturdays arrives Newcastle 10.50 am   p—pm

Full particulars of services in North Eastern England can be obtained on request at stations

Other communications regarding train services should be addressed to the District Passenger Superintendent, Newcastle

The train services shown here are subject to alteration or cancellation at short notice and do not necessarily apply at Bank and Public Holiday periods

BYE-LAWS AND REGULATIONS — GENERAL NOTICES, REGULATIONS AND CONDITIONS
Copies of the bye-laws and regulations will be found exhibited at stations

A booklet showing the conditions upon which tickets, including season tickets, are issued, and the regulations and conditions applicable to passengers' luggage, can be obtained, free of charge, from the station booking office.

NE 49

PUBLISHED BY THE RAILWAY EXECUTIVE (N.E. REGION) 19/51)   PRINTED IN GREAT BRITAIN   CHORLEY & PICKERSGILL LTD LEEDS

The last Public Timetable sheet published for the railway.   *Author*

Chapter Eleven
The Closure

In January 1939, when the debt to the LNER totalled more than £4500, an agreement re the working of the NSR by the main line company was arrived at as has already been recorded. This agreement lasted until 1948 when the LNER ceased to exist and was absorbed in the larger web of British Railways. In spite of all possible economies the NSR still made a loss and was faced with the problem of strengthening the trackwork to carry heavier locomotives and rolling stock required to replace their own worn out items. No means of overcoming this problem could be seen so, with the NSR owing them some £14,941, a memorandum proposing the closure of the NSR was sent by the North Eastern Region authorities to the Railway Executive. Among the reasons given for proposing the closure were, it is believed:

1 The cost of repairs to the NSR's locomotives was beyond the company's resources.
2 The coaching stock was in a condition commensurate with its age.
3 The track was only suitable for one class of BR North Eastern Region locomotive which was already considered obsolete.
4 The cost of putting the track into a state to take a locomotive of non-obsolete class would be at least £14,500.
5 The staff of 10 were not on a rate of pay, nor were their service conditions to the same general standards of the National Agreements.
6 The traffic on the line was diminishing with little prospect of a return to its former levels. Despite increasing rates and a generous treatment of the NSR's division of receipts, the need to strengthen the track to carry reasonably modern rolling stock and the further expense of the purchase of at least one locomotive, it was necessary to consider what effect the closing of the line would have on the earnings from such traffic that was passing.

At that time it is understood that BR's share of traffic to and from the line was £11,522, a decrease of some £3,414 from 1946.

The local bus services in the Seahouses area were operated by the United Automobile Services, a BTC company, and in 1948 it was operating a service between Chathill and Seahouses. It is assumed that British Railways felt that, if the line was closed and a co-ordinated rail-bus service was introduced, they would retain their share of the revenue. For parcels and goods traffic British Railways own road motor services from Belford and Chathill would meet all needs. These vehicles already did that task but picked up their load at Seahouses. Fish traffic did present a problem and British Railways realised that a considerable amount of this traffic would be lost to road haulage, similarly with inward coal traffic. The situation could be summarised thus:

1 If BR continued their agreement with the NSR they would be required to meet the railway's losses which could be as great as £2500 per year. They would continue to receive about £11,500 as gross contributory revenue.
2 If BR terminated the agreement they would be saved the burden of a loss of some £2500 a year and would lose some £4500 in contributory revenue whilst the receipts of the associated road companies would be expected to increase by some £1500 per year.

It was understood that the memorandum acknowledged that there was in the district a great deal of sentiment attaching to the rail link although of so simple a character. At the same time that sentiment had not been sufficient to maintain a railway, even one so simply equipped and so cheaply managed, in a state of solvency. Because expenditure on track and locomotives had to be faced in the immediate future, and in the absence of any indication of an increase in traffic receipts along with the simplicity of introducing alternative arrangements for a centre of population only four miles from a main line station, there was no justifiable case for the Railway Executive to continue assisting the NSR beyond the time needed for the establishment of alternative means of transport. As it would be wise to close the line before the 1948 fishing season it was recommended that six months' notice of termination of the agreement be given to the NSR who would then have to discharge their legal requirements. No doubt British Railways would give the company every assistance in the matter covering the period of the six months' notice.

Nothing happened from the submission of the Memorandum to the Railway Executive until early 1951, when the Executive decided to withdraw motive power from the line. The necessary arrangements were made and the impending closure attracted the attention of the popular press who gave considerable space to the news and published many photographs of the stock and staff. At 4.20 pm on Saturday 27th October, 1951, the little 'Y7' locomotive, British Railways No. 68089, left Seahouses bearing proudly the headboard proclaiming the train was "The Farne Islander". This last train left without ceremony but carried some fifty passengers including some of the original shareholders. The whistle blew to signal to the crossing keeper at North Sunderland to open the gates for the last time and the locomotive steamed into the station. Here no-one was about, not even a passenger, and with arrival at Chathill some fifteen minutes later, the train service of the North Sunderland Railway came to an end. After arriving at Chathill the coaches were shunted into the bay, then No. 68089 left the tracks of the NSR and travelled to Gateshead under its own steam; the last three trains scheduled for the day were worked by taxi – road transport had finally conquered.

The headboard "The Farne Islander" which was carried on the last journey was placed on the locomotive at Easter 1950 by the author when making a small cine film. The title was unofficial but did cause a deal of amusement to the regular travellers.

To replace the passenger trains the United Automobile Services allocated a bus to Seahouses to work a new schedule on the route from Seahouses to Alnwick via Chathill and Charlton. The pit in the engine shed was filled in and the sliding doors were removed to make a garage for it, the previous garage in the old chapel in North Street, North Sunderland had been closed for some time. Initially the bus more or less repeated the train service by making connections with the main line trains, but, as UAS got themselves organised, the service was integrated with their Alnwick–Seahouses–Bamburgh–Belford route. British Railways accelerated the Newcastle–Berwick trains and the buses no longer connected with every train. Chathill station is, however, one of the few stations to remain open on the east coast main line, albeit as an unstaffed halt.

At Seahouses the station buildings became the office of a British Railways/British Road Services joint agent, the former station master, whilst the goods warehouse was used by British Road Services who parked their lorries in the station yard at night. The warehouse was re-roofed with a peaked roof without any overhanging canopy. Part of the station yard was used as a builder's yard, the weighbridge and house were demolished. At North Sunderland the station buildings were used as a troop hut by the local Boy Scouts.

A meeting of the shareholders of the NSR was held in the Royal Hotel, Newcastle on 18th April, 1952. Afterwards, at an extra-ordinary general meeting, it was proposed and agreed to that the Company be registered as a Limited Liability Company under the Company's Act of 1948 thus allowing the Company to be liquidated and the assets sold up without the need for an Act of Parliament. The cost of seeking an Act would have been excessive therefore the pro-posal was accepted and on 25th April the North Sunderland Light Railway Company Limited was registered. As a result of this a wooden board was fixed to the British Railways' revenue account-ant's office in Neville Street, Newcastle proclaiming that it was the registered office of the Company. This was the first time the word "Light" appeared in the Company's title.

The winding-up of the Company was put to a general meeting on 23rd May and it was resolved that a petition be presented. The Winding-up Order was made on 16th June, the Board of Trade ap-pointed their Chief Official Receiver in London as Provisional Liqui-dator under the order who in turn appointed the Deputy Official Receiver in Newcastle to act.

The statement of affairs presented to the High Court of Justice Chancery Division by William Smith, Director, and Charles Norman Montague, Secretary on 11th August, 1952, it is understood, gave the total estimated assets as £2174. Against this were set the following liabilities:

Principal Creditor .... Rates £1
Loco hire, maintenance, tolls £23,128
Bondholder £407
Rent Charge Holders £159

giving an estimated deficiency as regards creditors of £21,521. As the issued capital was £24,820, the estimated deficiency as regards members was £46,341.

The Official Receiver's observations covered various factors of the Company's history and activities stating that passenger services began in October 1898 whereas all other sources state 18th December as the date. Audited and certified accounts for the years between 1937 and 1951 were quoted and in only two years, 1943 and 1944, did the railway work at a profit, £305 and £65 respectively. The value of the three coaches was given as a total of £80 and the station building, with fittings and furniture, as £200.

The failure of the Company could be attributed to the lack of available capital from the start for development purposes, the failure of Seahouses harbour to develop as a fishing port, and the failure to develop Seahouses as a holiday resort. It is ironical to state that the site of Seahouses station is now a car park which on most days in summer is completely filled. The Official Receiver agreed with these causes but did not consider the failure of the holiday resort as relevant.

The demolition of the railway started at Easter 1953 and took seven weeks, the contractors (the Motherwell Machinery and Scrap Company) using a small Ruston and Hornsby 48 hp diesel-mechanical locomotive and British Railways wagons. The demolition was thorough – little but the bridges and the track bed remain. The water tower at Long Nanny was cut up and the brick piers felled. At North Sunderland only the platform remains, the cottage has been pulled down and the crossing gates removed.

As mentioned above, the station yard at Seahouses is now a car park being completely cleared of all railway relics, but, if one looks carefully in the right place, it is possible to pick out some of the brickwork of the foundations of the station building. Between Seahouses and North Sunderland the track bed is now a public footpath.

Between the Pasture Hill bridge and the farmhouse a piggery has been built on the track bed, otherwise, apart from clearing the trees and bushes from the track, a new railway could be laid along the route.

So ends the history of the North Sunderland Railway, one of the struggling local independent railways that was passed by in groupings and yet was part of the railway scene of our country. In this day and age, when diesel electric traction and second class travel is universal on British Railways, it is pleasant to travel in reverie along the railway the author knew so well in his childhood when, in 1934, he first sampled the forms of travel which are so often thought to be a result of the British Railway's modernisation plan.

CHATHILL and SEAHOUSES—Weekdays
(Worked by North Sunderland Railway Company

DOWN

Distance M.C.		1 PASSENGER	2 PASSENGER	3 PASSENGER SO	4 PASSENGER	7 PASSENGER	8 PASSENGER	9 PASSENGER WSO	Sundays 1 PASSENGER	2 PASSENGER V	3 PASSENGER	5 PASSENGER	7 PASSENGER V
....	Chathill ......dep.	a.m. 8 14	a.m. 10 48	p.m. 12 42	p.m. 1 45	p.m. 5 42	p.m. 6 50	p.m 9 43	a.m 11 25	p.m. 1 40	p.m. 3 3	p.m. 7 47	p.m. 8 45
....	North Sunderland ,,	8 26	11 0	12 54	1 57	5 54	7 2	9 55	11 37	1 52	3 15	7 59	8 57
4 6	Seahouses ..arr.	8 29	11 3	12 57	2 0	5 57	7 5	9 58	11 40	1 55	3 18	8 2	9 0

V—Not after 5th September.

UP

Distance M.C.		1 PASSENGER	2 PASSENGER	3 PASSENGER SO	5 PASSENGER	7 PASSENGER	9 PASSENGER WSO	10 PASSENGER	Sundays 1 PASSENGER	2 PASSENGER V	3 PASSENGER	5 PASSENGER	6 PASSENGER V
....	Seahouses ..dep.	a.m. 7 48	a.m. 9 20	p.m. 12 10	p.m. 1 0	p.m. 4 10	p.m. 6 20	p.m. 9 15	a.m. 10 58	p.m. 1 13	p.m. 2 35	p.m. 7 22	p.m. 8 20
....	North Sunderland ,,	7 51	9 23	12 13	1 3	4 13	6 23	9 18	11 1	1 16	2 38	7 25	8 23
4 6	Chathill ..arr.	8 3	9 35	12 25	1 15	4 25	6 35	9 30	11 13	1 28	2 50	7 37	8 35

V—Not after 5th September.

Summer 1937 LNER Working Timetable.

Appendix One

Locomotives known to have worked on the NSR

Name or Number	Wheel Arrangement	Maker	Number	Year	Cyls	Wheel Diameter	Pressure	Tractive Effort	Weight	Remarks
Bamburgh	0–6–0ST ic	MW&Co.	1394	1898	12in. x 18in.	3ft 6in.	140 psi	8,640 lb.	25T app.	Scrapped 11.10.1949
The Lady Armstrong	0–4–0	AW&Co.	D25	1934	Diesel Electric	3ft 0in.	85 hp	8,000 lb.	15T 0C	Scrapped 11.10.1949
	0–4–0ST oc	MW&Co.	1074	1888	10in. x 16in.	2ft 9¾in.	120 psi	6,247 lb.		Whitaker Bros, Contractors
NER 407	0–6–0T ic	NER		1897	14in. x 20in.	3ft 6¼in.	140 psi	11,040 lb.	25T 0C	NER Cl. 'H2', LNER Cl. 'J79'
LNER 1787	0–6–0T ic	NER		1897	14in. x 20in.	3ft 6¼in.	140 psi	11,040 lb.	25T 0C.	LNER Cl. 'J79'
	0–4–0	AW&Co.		1933	Diesel Electric	2ft 9in.	95 hp	8,150 lb.	15T 0C	Armstrong Whitworth & Co. Demonstrator
LNER 81	0–4–0TG	Sentinel	7140	1927	6¾in. x 9in.	2ft 6in.	275 psi	12,600 lb. 4,705 lb.	20T 16C	LNER Cl. 'Y3'. Two-speed loco. Vac fitted
LNER 106	0–4–0TG	Sentinel	7838	1927	6¾in. x 9in.	2ft 6in.	275 psi	7,260 lb.	19T 16C	LNER Cl. 'Y1' Single speed loco
LNER 1690	0–6–0T ic	NER		1895	16in. x 22in.	4ft 7¼in.	140 psi	12,130 lb.	37T 12C	LNER Cl. 'J71' (NER Cl. 'E')

Drawing of locomotive *Bamburgh*.

Name or Number	Wheel Arrangement	Maker	Number Year Cyls	Wheel Diameter	Pressure	Tractive Effort	Weight	Remarks
LNER 986 (later 8089)	0–4–0T ic	LNER	1923 14in. x 20in.	3ft 6¼in.	140 psi	11,040 lb.	22T 14C	LNER Cl. 'Y7' British Railways 68089
LNER 982	0–4–0T ic	LNER	1923 14in. x 20in.	3ft 6¼in.	140 psi	11,040 lb.	22T 14C	LNER Cl. 'Y7' (NER Cl. 'H')
LMS 11217	0–4–0ST oc	L&YR	1895 13in. x 18in.	3ft 0⅜in.	160 psi	11,335 lb.	21T 5C	LMSR Cl. '0F' (L&Y Rly Cl. '21')
	4WD	R&H			48 hp			Motherwell Machinery & Scrap Co. Contractors.

Appendix Two

Coaching Stock owned by the NSR

NSR No.	Type	Seating Arrangement	Original Owner	No.	Type	Built	Bought	Remarks
	Five second-hand Highland Railways four-wheeled coaches		HR	103		1874	1898	Two made into wagons in 1911
			HR	106		1874	1898	Remaining two sold out of service in 1913
			HR	108		1874	1898	Sold out of service in 1913
			HR	109		1874	1898	
			HR	110		1874	1898	Converted by HR to brake compo in 1898

NSR No.	Type	Seating Arrangement	Original Owner	No.	Type	Built	Bought	Remarks
	5-compartment	4-wheeled 2F 1S 2T 50 seats	NER	1980	Diag. 58	1881	1911	Withdrawn 1938
	3-compartment	4-wheeled 3S Brake 30 seats	NER		Diag. X	1883	1912	Withdrawn 1934
3 (from 1943)	Saloon	4-wheeled S 30 seats Reduced to 20 when converted	NER		Diag. 61	1888	1924	Bought from Watts Hardy & Co. Converted to Brake Saloon in 1934. Withdrawn in 1951.
1 (from 1943)	6-compartment	6-wheeled 1F 1S 4T 60 seats	GER				1937	LNER 60883. Air brake only. Vac. pipe fitted in 1943. Withdrawn in 1951.
2 (from 1944)	6-compartment	6-wheeled 1F 1S 4T 60 seats	GER				1937	LNER 60916. Withdrawn in 1951
	3-compartment	6-wheeled 3T Brake	GER				1937	LNER 62305. Dual fitted. Withdrawn in 1939

Appendix Three

Timetables

1898

	am	am	pm	pm	pm	pm	pm
Seahouses	7.30	9.30	12.00	2.05	3.00	6.05	8.15
Chathill	7.45	9.45	12.15	2.20	3.15	6.20	8.30
Chathill	8.15	10.25	12.30	2.35	3.45	7.10	8.50
Seahouses	8.30	10.40	12.45	2.50	4.00	7.25	9.05

1915

	am	am	pm	pm	pm	pm
Seahouses	7.40		1.00	2.47		8.20
Chathill	7.55		1.15	3.02		8.35
Chathill	8.20	10.15	1.30	3.45	6.55	9.05
Seahouses	8.35	10.30	1.45	4.00	7.10	9.20

1938: Weekdays (Summer)

	am	am	pm	pm	pm	pm
Seahouses	7.40	9.20	1.00	4.10	6.20	9.15
Chathill	8.05	9.35	1.15	4.25	6.35	9.30
Chathill	8.14	10.46	1.45	5.42	6.50	9.43
Seahouses	8.29	11.01	2.00	5.57	7.05	9.58

Sundays

	am	pm	pm	pm	pm	pm
Seahouses	10.58	1.13	2.35	5.55	7.27	8.20
Chathill	11.13	1.28	2.50	6.10	7.43	8.35
Chathill	11.25	1.40	3.03	6.25	7.47	8.45
Seahouses	11.40	1.55	3.18	6.40	8.02	9.00

1951

	am	am	am	pm	pm	pm
Seahouses	7.35	9.15	10.10	12.50	4.40	6.45
Chathill	7.55	9.35	10.30	1.10	5.00	7.05
Chathill	8.10	9.40	10.50	1.50	5.50	7.20
Seahouses	8.30	10.00	11.10	2.10	6.10	7.40

Note:
The "up" trains ran from Seahouses to Chathill whilst "down" trains were from Chathill to Seahouses.

The slight variations of certain train times over the years is a reflection of alterations to main line trains between Newcastle and Berwick.